SharePoint 2013 Planet of the Apps v2.0

Legal

Contents

About the Author

Sahil Malik, is a techie like you. He loves new technologies, playing with gadgets, programming, building computer systems, or breaking them. He delivers trainings in Microsoft technologies, including SharePoint, and consults on various interesting projects around the world.

For his SharePoint trainings, or consulting work, you can find him on www.winsmarts.com.

@sahilmalik
facebook.com/sahilmalik

Preface

Welcome to Planet of the Apps v2.0. I had written the original Planet of the Apps right around SharePoint 2013 Beta2 came out. Since then SharePoint 2013 has changed, and I have changed. As I learn more, this awesome electronic medium is my opportunity to share updated content with you. So without much further ado, I present "Planet of the Apps v2.0". Here are some basic changes between v1 and v2.

a) **Full source code** – Many of you emailed me asking for source code. Well, it didn't make sense sharing beta code, it was going to change. At the end of this book, you can find the RTM version of the code used in this book.

b) **A full book** – I'll keep this one short, I got buried under paid work and could not dedicate enough time to write end to end treatise on SharePoint. It will happen one day, but until then I will instead publish full book-lets, not incomplete stories of yet unpublished stuff.

c) **Better Kindle Formatting** – Better, not perfect. The thing is, as awesome as Kindle is, it blows when it comes to formatting things such as source code. Written text should be fine. But the convenience and updateability of digital books is hard to beat. So I have included all the source code, the combination of text and source code I feel will give you the best of both worlds.

d) **A Pothole watch alert feature** – this is not a SharePoint feature. This is what I have found as things you need to be aware of in Apps. The thing is, a lot of folks out there are talking about Apps and relegating solutions to the heap of history. Microsoft isn't helping here either; they just said "Sandbox solutions are deprecated" which is the same company that told you "write a sandbox solution when you can". And then I hear word-smithing around the meaning of "deprecated". Here is how I understand "deprecated" – don't use it, we will remove it in next version. I don't think Apps are there yet, you can't do everything in apps or some things are done better in solutions, mostly farm solutions but sometimes even sandbox solutions. This leaves me confused, and I share some of my feelings on what I am doing as architectural choices in my projects to keep me future proof and safe going forward.

e) **Open Hole watch feature**, a list of things that I feel we will see solutions for in the current V2013 release, but guidance for this is not out yet.

f) **Continuous integration, uhh I mean improvement**. There will be a planet of the Apps v3.0 after this. Knowledge is not stagnant. I welcome your inputs and interaction, I learn as much from you – well who am I kidding. I learn more from you than you learn from me. Here is how you can reach out to me,

    a. **Twitter**: @sahilmalik
    b. **Facebook**: www.facebook.com/sahilmalik
    c. **Email**: www.winsmarts.com/contact.aspx

    Short of doing your project for you (for free), I welcome all sorts of engagement especially funny stuff.

Without much further ado, here's the tech stuff.

Introduction

You might have heard, Microsoft has gone app-solutely, app-sh!t on us in the 2013 release.

Perhaps the biggest change between SharePoint 2010 and SharePoint 2013, are apps. There is a pretty big reason why Microsoft is pushing us in this direction. The reason is - Microsoft likes money.

You think I am kidding. I am not.

See, the issue is, people put crap code in SharePoint. That prevents organizations from being able to upgrade SharePoint. Organizations can't upgrade SharePoint, they don't buy new SharePoint from Microsoft. Microsoft cries. Not good! This is what Microsoft is going to fix with Apps, by primarily keeping custom code far away from the SharePoint server, using Apps.

Also for shared scenarios, like Office 365, it is not practical to put code "in" the server. So in SharePoint 2010, Microsoft attempted to solve this problem by using Sandbox solutions. Sandbox solutions by their restrictive nature kept the server safe. But "restrictive" had another side to it – basic scenarios such as WebPart communication or being able to communicate with an external database required us to use complex workarounds. They made us unproductive. You could only do so much inside Sandbox solutions.

Then there was the issue of, an army of non-SharePoint developers that couldn't write anything for SharePoint, well, because they didn't know SharePoint or didn't want to learn it or perhaps they had a lot of existing investment in an alternative platform that was either cost or technology prohibitive in making work within SharePoint.

All that is changing with Apps. If you have skills such as ASPNET MVC, or put simply if that is what you prefer, you can write apps using your choice of technology. But you will see that sticking with Visual Studio templates is just a lot less hassle.

Apps are technically technology agnostic. But here is the real story,

a) As of now sticking with Visual Studio templates and ASP.NET technologies is just easier and more productive.
b) The one skill you will need to pick up for sure is JavaScript
c) And yes, you will need to still learn some basics about SharePoint especially if your App wants to leverage SharePoint facilities such as search, lists, taxonomy, etc.

The only most important thing you need to learn about Apps is, **Apps never run any code, EVER, on the SharePoint server.** An App's code can be client side, or optionally server side code. Both of them have the ability to talk with SharePoint using a well-defined permissions model.

In this book, you will learn about Apps, App architecture, fundamentals, App development life cycle and management. Unless and otherwise specified, all the details mentioned in this book apply to both SharePoint Foundation 2013 and SharePoint Server 2013. However, the examples described are created on SharePoint Server 2013. The primary difference you will find between SharePoint foundation and SharePoint server is that SharePoint server has a greatly expanded client object model and REST API, two technologies you will use a lot when writing Apps.

Apps is a pretty big topic though, and like any other big topic it is difficult to slice and dice it in a logical manner. So here is what I'm going to do,

a) Start with a basic theory about apps.
b) Then start explaining with a very basic example
c) Build upon that example bit by bit without overwhelming you with boring security related stuff
d) Once we know the fundamentals, I will get into security – you will see that in this logical progression its all actually very simple.

So lets get started with some basic theory.

Some basic theory about Apps

Well, first, what are apps? Apps are unique bits of software that end-users can download and install. They solve a specific need, they are somewhat isolated from each other, and they can interact with the host environment through a well-defined set of interfaces or API. For instance, the phone all on your mobile phone, can talk to contacts. There are concepts of security and permissions that also need to be considered here of course.

As far as I know, Apps were first popularized by smartphones. Users wanted to download and install a key functionality. One piece of software doing one job really well. They would download an app for it. Sometimes the app would ask for specific permissions, as a user of the App I could grant or deny such permissions. For instance if an App asked for access to my contacts, I can be pretty sure it was never accessing my GPS location.

The apps also had a marketplace, ratings, reviews, distribution model etc. It has been a very successful endeavor, but not until SharePoint 2013 has anyone attempted to introduce it to the enterprise. Introduce it to the enterprise such as a SharePoint intranet full of useful apps.

Not until SharePoint 2013 has anyone tried to introduce apps to the enterprise. Apps use SharePoint as a 'host' or 'glue' that brings these apps together. They have a light foot print on SharePoint and when uninstalled they clean up nicely after them.

Apps, the Golden List

I put together a list of things you must know about Apps. This list, well, read it well. Read it thoroughly. Write it on the walls of your shower if that helps. If someone pinches you at 3AM when you're in deep sleep, you should be able to recite this list orally.

Here are some key points about Apps to remember.

a) Apps never run any code on the SharePoint server.

b) Apps are downloaded and installed. They can be obtained from an app store (corporate catalog or public) or deployed using API or PowerShell.

c) In the UI, SharePoint lists are also apps – well they are not apps underneath the scenes. They are SharePoint lists and document libraries just like they have always been. Calling them apps is a matter of pandering to user convenience or perhaps confusing them – time will tell.

d) An installed App runs from a URL other than SharePoint. By default any app will run full screen – that is it takes over your entire page with a link to get back to your SharePoint site. But it can also run as an IFRAME, or can be launched via a CustomAction in the Hostweb. When launched as a custom action, it can launch itself as a dialog or as a full page.

e) As I mentioned above, an App always runs from a URL other than the SharePoint site. App security relies on this tenet, you should not try to get around this.

f) Where the app is installed, is called "HostWeb". Optionally, an app may provision a subweb, which is called the "AppWeb". AppWeb lives under the HostWeb, but at a completely different URL. Therefore the IFRAME is effectively showing a site from a URL different from the host web – this prevents XSS attacks. There is however a well-defined mechanism allowing the App to talk to the parent HostWeb and vice versa.

g) Even if the App is not running out of an AppWeb, it is still running on a completely different URL (okay I think I've driven this point enough).

h) The AppWeb can optionally have server side storage. This storage can be in a SharePoint list or somewhere else or a hybrid approach using both.

i) That somewhere else in the point above, can also have server side code, except such server side code cannot run on the SharePoint server where the app was installed from.

j) This server side code, or client side code can interact with HostWeb via well-defined APIs and permissions based on OAuth. These permissions must be granted ahead of time. Apps are authenticated into SharePoint, Office 365 apps use Azure ACS, On-Premises apps use S2S (server to server) trust. There is a pretty good chance that we will see the ability to setup On-Premises SharePoint installations with Azure ACS as well down the road.

k) The server side code can be written in a non-SharePoint technology, or even a non-Microsoft technology.

Did you read the above? Not speed read, but actually read! You know I'm counting on you to read the above.

How exciting! But, I'm sure you are both intrigued and full of questions at this point!

1. The app runs from a separate URL? How does it look or feel like part of the SharePoint site is running in? What if your app is installed in many environments? What if it is running both as an IFRAME and full screen?

    a. The answer is, Microsoft has given us something called as a chrome control. A chrome control brings in all the styles from the SharePoint site the app is running in into the App.

b. **POTHOLE ALERT**: I feel Apps (and SharePoint 2013 in general) is UI challenged. The guidance beyond using Chrome control is quite minimal. While some may argue the flexibility this offers, I feel this will lead to different organizations creating different shaped wheels and resulting in an inconsistent user experience between apps.

c. **POTHOLE ALERT**: Another issue I see is, highly branded sites, especially those that completely kill out of the box SharePoint styles might find themselves seriously affecting the intended UI of the App. When branding a SharePoint 2013 site, I'd first ask – do you really have to do it? I mean, can't you achieve very close to the same look and feel using the much improved out of the box theming support? And if you must brand, well, you'd better test it with a multitude of Apps. I'm afraid I don't have a better answer.

2. If the App is running on a different domain, how does it make a cross-domain request back into SharePoint?

a. The answer is, SharePoint comes with support for secure cross domain calls. These calls can come from both client side or server side – even though the mechanism client side and server side code use is quite different, they both obey a permissions model that Apps architecture is baked with.

b. **POTHOLE ALERT**: I must say, Apps permissions are impressive, a lot of thought and intelligence has gone into making all this work. However, as developers of Apps, especially Apps acquired from the marketplace, and provider hosted apps require you to think of Apps somewhat differently than apps on your phone. I will share more thoughts on this as the book progresses.

c. **POTHOLE ALERT**: Apps make me 'appy. They keep my SharePoint server safe, and they ensure that my future upgrades will be relatively painless. However, in reality in writing a lot of reusable apps, especially what those targeted towards the marketplace, I found myself requiring to grant "FullControl" permission. Well, that's crAppy, isn't it? Does this mean I don't like Apps? You're Appsolutely mistaken. I love apps. I just feel it needs to mature further to deliver on it's true promise of potential.

3. If my app involves a server other than SharePoint, and there is server side code, how does it authenticate back into SharePoint? Who installs this code when the app gets installed?

   a. The answer is, Office 365 apps use Azure ACS/OAuth, and on-premises apps use S2S (server to server) trust or Azure ACS/OAuth. Any user that has the permissions that the app is asking for can install the app. There are some special cases such as App only permission policy, and On the Fly permissions that maybe exceptions to this rule.

4. How does the app get access to the SharePoint API?

   a. Using client object model and Rest API. If you're a CSOM/REST API God, you're by defacto an App-God. Corollary, if you're a CSOM/REST duffer, you're a complete Dumbapp.

5. Do I have to have server side code?
    a. You don't have to have server side code, it is optional depending upon the functionality. Later on in this book, you will see something called "SharePoint hosted app". A SharePoint hosted app can use only client side code. So, sometimes I ask myself, If I am writing a SharePoint hosted App, why not just write a Sandbox solution? The answer is, Sandbox solutions don't give you an app permission module, or app redistribution model, but sandbox solutions can run limited server side code.

6. Since the App runs in an IFRAME, how big is that IFRAME? Can it look/feel like a WebPart? Or is it something else?
    a. By default an App will support full page experience, or rather you have to put in extra work to prevent a full page experience. Optionally you can have a client WebPart experience, or launch from within SharePoint using a custom action experience.
    b. **POTHOLE ALERT**: Put this in the same category as UI challenges, what I found is that writing the same code so it can in both in an IFRAME and a full page required me to follow a certain design pattern. I describe this technique later on the book.

7. How can I be sure that the app I am installing won't bring the international space station down?
    a. Apps request for specific permissions. The SharePoint product team has been careful enough to not include such permissions.

The international space station, let's hope has been smart enough to not run SharePoint up there. Either way, as an author of an app you can restrict your app to stay under a permission set.

Kinds of apps

As you can see, there are so many choices when authoring an app. While this gives us plenty of architectural choice, it does make it a bit difficult to categorize them. At a very high level, you can consider three ways to categorize apps.

a) What is the app scoped to.
b) How users access the app
c) Where is the app hosted?

And as far as the scoping of the app, you have two choices here,

a) Web Scope – where you install the App in your SPWeb. It can use the resources of the parent web. This is an example of an app that can be a SharePoint-hosted app.
b) Tenant Scope – is shared between many consumers. The app can partition experience and data per consumer. It is installed once and shared many times. Usually such apps by definition have a hosted backend, and therefore are unsuitable for SharePoint-hosted apps.

As far as how do users access the app, you have three choices,

a) Full page immersive apps – every app needs to provide this experience. In short, the app's IFRAME takes over the entire page. Yes you do have to follow some UI guidelines though, such as having a back button is a requirement etc. But the App itself takes the whole page.

b) App Part – this is a client side WebPart that shows the App in an IFRAME that takes over a small portion of the page.

c) Extension App –accessed by clicking on a link or an ECB menu.

As far as where is the App Hosted, you have three choices,

1. SharePoint Hosted
2. Server hosted
    a. Provider Hosted
    b. Autohosted

SharePoint Hosted Apps

An App that is served out of the same SharePoint installation as where SharePoint is installed and has no other server side component, is called as a SharePoint hosted App. When you install such an App, you install it in a SPWeb. A child SPWeb is created for you. The SPWeb you installed the App in is called as the HostWeb. The SPWeb that got created because you installed the App is called as the AppWeb. Even though this AppWeb is a child SPWeb, you cannot see it in the UI, and you cannot find it on the same URL as the HostWeb. You have to go through some steps ahead of time in setting up your SharePoint installation so such URLs can be provisioned on the fly. You will find more details on such setup in my book on setting up your SharePoint dev machine at **http://bit.ly/spdevmachine**

Server Hosted App

If your App needs any server side code, for instance if it needs to run an action not prompted by the user, or to perform elevation scenarios, you will need server side code. In this scenario, it's obvious that you will probably involve technologies other than JavaScript running on the server. The question here is, who installs and sets up this server. Here also, there are two categories, provider hosted apps – where you the app author installs the server, or Autohosted apps, where the installation of the App results in a server side area being provisioned for you in Azure.

Server Hosed App – provider hosted

I call this BYOS, bring your own server. Here, you, the App developer sets up and installs the server side area. This gives you immense flexibility in how a single server installation can partition it's view/data across multiple app installations, or the choice of technologies on the server side. But the obvious disadvantage here is, well you have to setup the server, and figure out all the "trust" issues between SharePoint and this server ahead of time. In Azure ACS/Office 365 it's not such a problem, but in S2S on-premises installations this will require you to create and install a certificate, and run some PowerShell scripts and create something called as issuer ID and client ID. If you're a large enough vendor creating apps for lots of customers, you can also facilitate the discovery of your app's security related details – but my point here is, this approach of a server hosted app is a little more headache and work for you – at the tradeoff of more functionality.

OPEN HOLE: Provider hosted apps can be used for Office 365 or On Premises. But currently there is no guidance available on setting up OAuth for on-premises SharePoint installation. This means, for on-premises, the process of installing an app will require some extra work from you.

Server hosted App – Autohosted

There is a state in America called New Jersey. We like to poke fun at New Jersey for various reasons, but one of those many reasons is that it's bars have a BYOB policy (bring your own booze policy) in some bars. That has advantages of course, but the obvious disadvantage is more work and planning on our part. The autohosted app is the exact opposite of it. You simply install the App, and with the installation of the App a server side area gets provisioned in Azure. When the App gets uninstalled this azure hosted area disappears. Obviously you don't have the same level of flexibility here as a provider hosted app, but in many scenarios, the lesser overhead/headache of this option makes it worth a look. And obviously this azure hosted area is going to cost you a bit. How much? We don't know yet, but Microsoft will release details on this sometime soon.

POTHOLE ALERT: One big limitation of autohosted apps is that each app installation provisions an autohosted area. You can't say "Hey just go ahead and reuse this existing area". This means, partitioning views on common data requires some thought on your side. Secondly, and this is not such a pothole, but something to consider – this Azure hosted area is something that Office 365 and SharePoint pre-negotiated upon. Its not something that you will see in your Azure portal that you can tweak or configure. It's a black box.

OPEN HOLE: At the time of writing this book, the following things are unclear about autohosted apps

a) How much is it going to cost?
b) Will it work with on-premises solutions – at the current time it is not possible.
c) What will be the development story if indeed these autohosted apps are going to cost. In many scenarios, you can't take S2S code and use it in auto hosted scenarios without any changes.

Also remember, an autohosted or provider hosted app, can also optionally provision an AppWeb – this is a hybrid of SharePoint hosted and Server hosted.

Now I know you're itching to open Visual Studio and etch what you have read so far in your mind. Patience SPGrassHopper, lets first understand a pedantic comparison of farm solutions versus sandbox solutions vs. apps.

Farm Solutions / Sandbox Solutions / Apps

Conventional SharePoint development talks about .wsps. Solution packages – deployed either as farm solutions or sandbox solutions. SharePoint 2010 introduced new solution types called *sandbox solutions* apart from the *farm solutions* you are aware of in MOSS 2007 and WSS 3.0. SharePoint 2013 introduced this new type of solution called "*Apps for SharePoint*" and now you have three different sort-of solutions. While each one of them has their own pros and cons, here below is the table that gives you a high level information and comparison about these solution types.

Farm Solution	Sandbox Solution	Apps for SharePoint
Introduced in WSS 3.0/MOSS 2007	Introduced in SharePoint 2010	Introduced in SharePoint 2013
Significant customizations to SharePoint are possible via this approach	Limited customizations to SharePoint are possible via this approach	The level of customization introduced depends on permissions for the app. But they are still not as powerful as a farm solution.
Full trust	Partially trusted	Trust can be

Solutions	solutions	manageable
Developed in house or acquire from 3rd party providers	Developed in house or acquire from 3rd party providers	Developed in house or acquire from 3rd party providers
Only suitable for on-premise deployments	On-Premise or cloud	On-Premise or cloud
Solution contains solution manifest file, features, templates, assemblies etc.	Solution contains solution manifest file, features, templates, assemblies etc.	App contains App manifest, feature and elements manifest, pages and images etc.
Has an upgrade story, but relies on the developer for cleanup	Has an upgrade story, but relies on the developer for cleanup	The upgrade story is much cleaner
Can contain code behind files	Can contain code behind files for only site pages	Cannot contain code-behind pages where the code-behind may run in SharePoint
Fully supports Server side, Client side object model	Partially supports server side, client side object model	Supports only client side object model. Server side code runs on a server other than SharePoint
Managed by Farm Administrators	Managed by farm and site collection admins	Managed by farm and site collection admins
Monitored by	Monitored by	Monitored by

Farm Administrators	Farm Administrators and Site Collection administrators	Farm Administrators and Site Collection administrators
Essential to have SharePoint development skills	Essential to have SharePoint development skills	Simplistic apps can get away with very limited SharePoint skills. Even when you do need SharePoint skills, it isn't to the level of Farm solutions.

The above comparison should give you a clear picture that apps differ in architecture with farm or sandbox solutions.

You may ask, what this means for us SharePoint developers practically speaking!

Apps, the practical view

Warning, this section is loaded with personal opinions. My feeling is, Apps will be the majority of code we will write. There is so much that the client object model and REST API in SharePoint 2013 expose that I see very little need to write farm solutions, and almost no need to author sandbox solutions. With that said, let me first describe some borderline scenarios where you would want to still use sandbox solutions.

1. Sandbox solutions run in a monitored sandbox. Nothing prevents an app from hammering your server

with a while (true) {runslowconsumptionofCPU();} sort of code.

2. Branding etc. is perhaps going to be easier using sandbox solutions, you can declaratively provision a master page, and easily swap the SPWeb's master page. Apps can do the same with the client object model, but it will feel a bit more cumbersome because it will have to be done through authenticated code, not CAML.

3. Sandbox solutions will be a bit more self-contained than the app. Again branding is a good example, once the HostWeb is branded, the AppWeb has no use. It sticks around like a useless male angler fish after it has mated.

4. There are some scenarios that I couldn't do using Apps but they were so easy to do using Sandbox solutions. If you find a solution to these please give me a shout out. But when I wanted to create a content type where I wanted to control the content type id, apps left me hanging. Or when I wanted to deploy a custom activity for sharepoint workflow, I had to deploy it using a sandbox solution. Or if I wanted to find the URLs of lists and libraries in the HostWeb at runtime, well it wasn't possible unless I gave FullControl to the App, which sort of sucks.

That said, the above arguments are weak! The advantages Apps provide you almost make Sandbox solutions deprecated. MSDN in fact says they are deprecated – that is quite a strong word though. They will still work, they are just not the preferred way of writing code. The sad thing of course is that Microsoft told us at the release of SharePoint 2010 that sandbox solutions were the holy-grail. Now they tell us, they are deprecated. The good news is, if you wrote code using sandbox solutions, you are looking forward to a really boring, eventless upgrade to SharePoint 2013. You do want to play with the latest version, don't you?

Bottom line – try very hard to write an App instead of a sandbox solution. Sometimes it takes me longer to achieve the same thing using an App versus a sandbox solution, I try and explain to the client why writing an App is a better, more future proof choice. If they still insist on a sandbox solution, well at least I sleep guilt free.

Now, let's talk about farm solutions. My IT Pro brethren (also known as IT Ogres) will get mad at me when I say this, but sorry Farm solutions are still not disposable. There are just too many scenarios where you will need to resort to farm solutions, here are some that I could think off of the top of my head,

1. Custom Document ID generators
2. Custom Barcode/label generation
3. Custom expiration actions and formulae
4. User profile synch in WAN/high latency environments
5. Sitemapproviders, though who the hell uses these anyway, except OOTB SharePoint. And OOTB SharePoint navigation in SharePoint 2013 rocks – it can even go across site collections now.
   a. **POTHOLE ALERT**: Cross site publishing is highly reliant on search, this means there is a delay between the page being published and the page being visible.
   b. **POTHOLE ALERT**: The above pothole is not such a big deal, but the bigger deal I feel, is discovery of newer managed properties that cross site publishing relies on full crawls. This is sometimes very inconvenient on internet facing sites.
6. Custom auditing
7. Custom people pickers, especially when you are using a custom IP-STS (this is a big one).

All said and done, Apps will be the majority of business code you will write, but you will still need some farm solutions, albeit a lot lesser. If your IT Ogre is being difficult, well feel free to beat him with this ebook.

POTHOLE ALERT: Anyway, the thing is, your IT Ogre has a point. Farm solutions in SharePoint 2010 could be restricted using CAS policies. But c'mon let's be honest, we just put stuff in the GAC, where it ran under full trust anyway. Now, if you're thinking you were smart and painfully wrote CAS policies, please carefully observe the following tweet,

Sahil Malik
@sahilmalik

#SP2013 runs everything under <trust legacyCasModel="true" level="Full"/>, which means partial-trust appdomains run under full trust.

← Reply ⭢ Retweet ★ Favorite

9:25 AM - 8 Dec 12 · Embed this Tweet

Oooh! Not feeling so smart anymore are you? The thing is, in SharePoint 2013, all code, CAS policy or not, runs under full trust. Your CAS policies are ignored. Ouch! Write Apps buddy.

App lifecycle

There are primarily 5 steps in an app for SharePoint lifecycle. Finding the app, installing or upgrading the app, update app (only in development environment), Uninstall app and remove the app. Apps for SharePoint can be searched and found from the app catalog or SharePoint store. If you have an App package available, it can be installed or further upgraded on changes or enhancements. Apps designed and developed by developers can be installed and later updated. When the app is no longer required, it can be uninstalled and removed from the catalog after uninstallation.

Apps that are SharePoint hosted and run under the app web context require configuration to your SharePoint development environment that I will discuss shortly, but let's get our feet wet and hands dirty by writing our first SharePoint app.

Writing your First App – The Appetizer

Appetizer, LOL, I'm so funny. Well, this is a very simple App that will get our toes wet with writing apps, a little taste-test of what Apps are. I'm going to walk you through the process of first writing a simple SharePoint app, installing it, and running it. In the process you will also get a behind the scenes look at how the App is run and installed on your SharePoint server.

But before you dive into the exercise, can you please read the "Golden List" section one more time please.

Done reading? Okay let's get rolling!

Begin Exercise: Appetizer

Start Visual Studio 2012, and create a new SharePoint 2013 app as shown below,

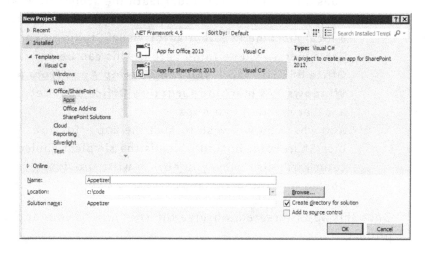

Choose to create a SharePoint hosted app as shown below,

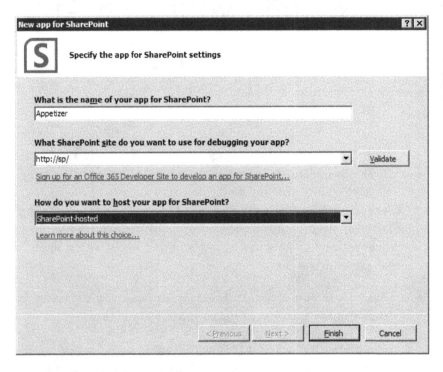

Here, Visual Studio wishes to know,

a) The name of your App
b) Where will you install and debug it. Visual Studio does a bunch of tricks underneath the scenes to make it easy for us to debug our apps, so this URL, usually a local machine is essential for Visual Studio to know. The super awesome thing here is, this can be an Office 365 site too – **you can develop Apps from a Windows 7/8 machine targeting Office 365**. Yet another reason I like Apps.
c) And where do you wish to host the app – for now pick SharePoint hosted which is the simplest choice. Later I will also show you how to write provider hosted or autohosted apps.

Once this app is created, observe the structure of your app project,

```
▲  ⊞ Appetizer
   ▲  📁 Features
      ▷  S Feature1
   ▲  📁 Package
      ▷  🎁 Package.package
   ▲  🗐 Content
         📄 App.css
         🔖 Elements.xml
   ▲  🗐 Images
         🖼 AppIcon.png
         🔖 Elements.xml
   ▲  🗐 Pages
         🌐 Default.aspx
         🔖 Elements.xml
   ▲  🗐 Scripts
         🗎 _references.js
         🗎 App.js
         🔖 Elements.xml
         🗎 jquery-1.7.1.intellisense.js
         🗎 jquery-1.7.1.js
         🗎 jquery-1.7.1.min.js
      🔖 AppManifest.xml
      🗏 packages.config
```

You will note that this app includes a solution package and a feature, and it looks like it is deploying a feature into an SPWeb. Using this feature, it deploys various modules, and those modules seem to deploy an aspx (Default.aspx), and some JavaScript and css files.

For instance, open the Pages\Element.xml file, it should contain code as shown below,

```
<?xml version="1.0" encoding="utf-8"?>
<Elements
xmlns="http://schemas.microsoft.com/sharepoi
nt/">
<Module Name="Pages">
<File Path="Pages\Default.aspx"
Url="Pages/Default.aspx" />
</Module>
</Elements>
```

AHA! What is that Module tag? In fact, what is the generic name for all this XML goo?

As a SharePoint developer, you need to be familiar with all this XML goo. The technical word for this XML goo is CAML or Collaborative Application Markup Language. CAML is to SharePoint what SQL is to databases. It is used to describe data, and query data. Over here, we are describing data.

Specifically we are getting familiarized with a specific CAML element called "Module". Module has the responsibility of picking up a file from the feature, and dropping it in the content database. Therefore in this scenario, the file being picked up is default.aspx from the pages folder, and it is being dropped in the content database at Pages\Default.aspx. But remember, all this is tied to a feature, and the feature gets activated in the AppWeb. So all these app related artifacts are in the AppWeb.

I leave it up to you to examine what else is contained in this solution package and feature – you should find the following,

a) The Default.aspx which is the launch page for the app
b) The App.js file which contains the JavaScript logic
c) A bunch of references to a few jQuery files for supporting code
d) An "AppIcon.png" file deploying the icon for the app.
e) An App.css file that has custom styles for our app.

If you open that Default.aspx, you should see code as shown below,

```
<!-- Add your CSS styles to the following file -->
<link rel="Stylesheet" type="text/css" href="../Content/App.css" />

<!-- Add your JavaScript to the following file -->
<script type="text/javascript" src="../Scripts/App.js"></script>
</asp:Content>
<%-- The markup and script in the following Content element will be placed in the <body> of the page --%>
<asp:Content ContentPlaceHolderID="PlaceHolderMain" runat="server">

    <div>
        <p id="message">
            <!-- The following content will be replaced with the user name when you run the app - see App.js -->
            initializing...
        </p>
    </div>

</asp:Content>
```

So we have a "p" tag with id=message. And we are referencing a javascript file called App.js. Above in this aspx, also note that we have included jQuery and some SharePoint specific files. Interestingly the files are debug versions – before you deploy such an app into production, you should remove the .debug portion in the files so minified versions of your App download.

POTHOLE ALERT: I'm pretty sure many of Apps will be deployed using .debug versions. Not good.

POTHOLE ALERT: I <u>really</u> dislike the mechanism using which the default Visual Studio templates have included jQuery. This is for two reasons,

a) They have hardcoded the jQuery version to 1.7. Future jQuery versions will have breaking changes, and frankly the world will move on, many SharePoint branding artifacts that many customers will end up using will use newer versions of jQuery. Newer versions in the same scope will override older versions – your app might break.

b) Why oh why did they include jQuery in the global scope!? They should have created the $ variable in your App's scope so it never interfered with the global scope. This way, you'd be version agnostic and live side by side. I highly suggest getting really good at JavaScript before diving too deep into an App project.

I can perhaps understand why they did this, to make the starter code more understandable, but you as a developer should remember to write good JavaScript code.

Now, open App.js and observe the code as shown below,

```
var context;
var web;
var user;

// This code runs when the DOM is ready and creates a context object which is needed to use the SharePoint object model
$(document).ready(function () {
    context = SP.ClientContext.get_current();
    web = context.get_web();

    getUserName();
});

// This function prepares, loads, and then executes a SharePoint query to get the current users information
function getUserName() {
    user = web.get_currentUser();
    context.load(user);
    context.executeQueryAsync(onGetUserNameSuccess, onGetUserNameFail);
}

// This function is executed if the above OM call is successful
// It replaces the contents of the 'helloString' element with the user name
function onGetUserNameSuccess() {
    $('#message').text('Hello ' + user.get_title());
}

// This function is executed if the above call fails
function onGetUserNameFail(sender, args) {
    alert('Failed to get user name. Error:' + args.get_message());
}
```

In this code, we are making a CSOM call and fetching the currently logged in user's identity. Go ahead and hit "F5" to run the app, at this point Visual studio will automatically package and deploy the app for you in SharePoint.

Once the app is loaded, verify that the app runs in the browser as shown below.

Appetizer

Hello Administrator

Leave the app running, let's do some detective work. Look at the URL of the app, .. it should look as follows,

http://ws-d21e0710089a8f.apps.ws.int/
Appetizer/Pages/Default.aspx?
SPHostUrl=http%3A%2F%2Fsp&
SPLanguage=en%2DUS&
SPClientTag=0&
SPProductNumber=15%2E0%2E4420%2E1017&
SPAppWebUrl=http%3A%2F%2Fws%2Dd21e0710089a8f%2Eap
ps%2Ews%2Eint%2FAppetizer

The URL above contains,

a) The tenant ws
b) The app domain: apps.ws.int
c) The SubWeb URL: Appetizer
d) QueryString parameters – double click the AppManifest.xml file you will see the "StartPage" is defined as the /pages/default.aspx file, but it has a QueryString called "{StandardTokens}" which gets replaced with all the querystring parameters above. There are many other such querystring parameters and URL tokens, please see the SharePoint App replacement parameters section later in the book.

Don't stop debugging yet, keep the app running, and open SharePoint 2013 management shell, and run the following commands to verify that Appetizer is indeed a subsite of http://sp

```
Administrator: SharePoint 2013 Management Shell
PS C:\Users\administrator> $site = Get-SPSite http://sp
PS C:\Users\administrator> $site.RootWeb.Webs

Url
---
http://ws-d21e0710089a8f.apps.ws.int/Appetizer

PS C:\Users\administrator> _
```

Now check out the folders in the appWeb,

```
Administrator: SharePoint 2013 Management Shell
PS C:\Users\administrator> $appWeb = $site.RootWeb.Webs[0]
PS C:\Users\administrator> $appWeb.Folders | ft Url

Url
---
images
_vti_pvt
Lists
Scripts
Pages
Content
_catalogs
_private

PS C:\Users\administrator> _
```

Note that the folders Scripts, Pages, and Content are created using modules using the feature that is packed into the app.

Next, verify the files in the Scripts folder,

```
Administrator: SharePoint 2013 Management Shell
PS C:\Users\administrator> $scripts = $appWeb.Folders[3]
PS C:\Users\administrator> $scripts.Files | ft Url

Url
---
Scripts/App.js
Scripts/jquery-1.7.1.intellisense.js
Scripts/jquery-1.7.1.min.js
Scripts/jquery-1.7.1.js

PS C:\Users\administrator> _
```

Note that these are the same files that are present in the Scripts module in your Visual Studio project.

Now stop debugging Visual Studio. Visual Studio will retract and uninstall your App – you will see that the App is gone, as if it was never there, much cleaner than solution packages.

Next, in Visual Studio, right click and choose publish, once the app is published, make a copy of it, and rename the copy to .zip extension, and double click on it to open it. You will note that it is just a .zip file that contains a .wsp file as shown below,

You can at this point also rename the .wsp to .cab and open it to view the contents inside.

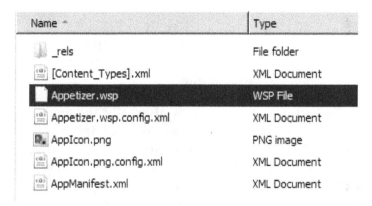

You can think of the entry point to the App as the AppManifest.xml file – this is what tells SharePoint what the app is all about. If you double click on it, Visual Studio will give you a nice windows form to maintain this xml file. But I'd like you to open it in Notepad r right click\view code. It will look like as below,

```xml
<?xml version="1.0" encoding="utf-8" ?>
<!--Created:cb85b80c-f585-40ff-8bfc-12ff4d0e34a9-->
<App xmlns="http://schemas.microsoft.com/sharepoint/2012/app/manifest"
     Name="Appetizer"
     ProductID="{a0d1d80c-c65a-4781-9f8c-bc5bfe1d1b19}"
     Version="1.0.0.0"
     SharePointMinVersion="15.0.0.0"
>
  <Properties>
    <Title>Appetizer</Title>
    <StartPage>~appWebUrl/Pages/Default.aspx?{StandardTokens}</StartPage>
  </Properties>

  <AppPrincipal>
    <Internal />
  </AppPrincipal>

</App>
```

Next, find the .app file, and visit your app catalog site, it should be at http://sp/apps/catalog. Under "Apps for SharePoint" upload this .app file.

NOTE: Do you not see an App catalog? Did the app not get installed properly on your machine, or are the URLs different? Well, running Apps requires some initial app related setup. This is described in my SP Dev Machine book at http://bit.ly/spdevmachine.

Next, visit the http://sp site and choose to add an app,

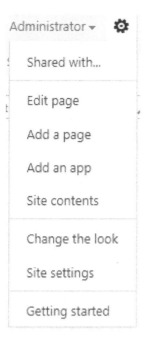

Find the Appetizer app as shown below,

You will be presented with a dialog to trust this app as shown below,

Click on "Trust it",

The app will now install

And a few moments later ..

YAY!

Once the app is installed, click on it to visit it, verify that the functionality works as before.

Now, run Fiddler, and hit F5 one more time, observe the authentication mechanism. You would note the user downloads the app and SharePoint authenticates the user.

Also note the call to CSOM. You would note a header by the name of X-RequestDigest.

This is to avoid Cross-Site request attacks. For instance, clicking on a button in domain1, could cause a post to domain2. The user gets authenticated automatically to domain2. But, let's say, the post request was to delete something (like in SharePoint deleteweb.aspx for instance), the user would get authenticated and delete the web. That is obviously not good.

To protect against this, SharePoint requests that **you send the form digest with every request that can edit data on the server**. This is called as the X-RequestDigest. CSOM API does this automatically and server side code will call ValidateFormDigest to ensure that the request is valid. REST API requires you to get the X-FormDigest first using a call to /_api/ContextInfo, this is described in an example later.

End Exercise: Appetizer

App Deployment

Congratulations. You just wrote your first app. Now that you have this app written, how can you make it available to end users? You have four choices!

1. The SharePoint Public App store, maintained by Microsoft. App Developers can upload an app, and have a payment model as the app is installed and used. You do have some restrictions on the kinds of apps you can upload here though. For instance, apps that request full control cannot be put on the App store.

2. Through a deployment API, which is what Visual Studio used when you deployed the app. You can also use PowerShell.

3. You can upload directly from the UI in a developer site as well, but in other kinds of sites end users do not add apps to catalogs, they install apps that are already available. End users can request apps that can then be added to the app catalog by administrators. The process of uploading and using an app in the developer site is as follows,

Begin Exercise: Using the Developer Site

a. Provision a developer site, this is a site definition you can use.

b. Find a link on the home page called "new app to deploy"

c. Upload the app as shown below, I assume your App is called "HelloWorldApp.app",

d. Choose to deploy the app as shown below,

e. You will be asked to trust the app per the permissions the app requires,

f. Wait for the app to get installed

to,

g. Next, click on the app link in site contents, and you should see the app running.

End Exercise: Using the Developer Site

4. The fourth possible way of deploying and using apps is the enterprise catalog. There will be many examples where customers will want to have their "internal app store". There can be many reasons for

this, perhaps they do not want their applications on the internet app store or perhaps they do not want to go through the approval process. Or sometimes, the environment is really secure and has no internet access. Either way, the need for a corporate app catalog is a very real need. I described this in the Appetizer section, but the below exercise illustrates those steps clearly,

Begin Exercise: Using the Corporate App Catalog

The first thing you will need to enable the enterprise app catalog, is to actually create it. In order to do so, visit Central Administration, and under the "Apps" section look for the "Manage App Catalog" link.

Apps

- **SharePoint and Office Store**
  Purchase Apps | Manage App Licenses | Configure Store Settings

- **App Management**
  Manage App Catalog | Monitor Apps | Configure App URLs | App Permissions

The first time you visit this link, you will be asked to either manage an existing app catalog, or create a new app catalog. Creating a new app catalog is a matter of creating a site collection based on the app catalog site definition.

Once such an app catalog is created, visit it, and look for a link called "Apps for SharePoint"

Libraries

Lists

Recent

    App Requests

    Apps for Office

    Apps for SharePoint

Site Contents

Clicking on that link, will take you to a document library called "AppCatalog" where you can upload an app file. Go ahead and upload the HelloWorldApp.App app that we created earlier.

The interesting thing here is that during the upload process, the page will let you customize many aspects of the app's discoverability experience. It's icon, name, description, and whether it appears in the featured/noteworthy section at top or not.

Once you have uploaded your app, visit http://sp, and click on the "Site Contents" menu on the left. Here, choose to add an app, and you should be able to see your HelloWorldApp app in the list of available apps you can add, as shown below,

Go ahead and click on the HelloWorldApp app. Just like before, you will be shown a dialog asking for trust,

Do you trust HelloWorldApp?   ✕

Let it access basic information about this site.

Let it access basic information about the users of this
site.

HelloWorldApp

| Trust It | Cancel |

Click on "Trust it" and wait for a few seconds for the app to
be installed. It takes a few seconds because it has to create
the AppWeb SPWeb, and the associated app artifacts in it.
When the app is ready to use, it will look like as shown
below,

Clicking on the app icon will run the app as before. Once
installed, the app is very similar to the app you created and
installed via the deployment API.

End Exercise: Using the Corporate App Catalog

Congratulations, you've written and deployed an app. At this
time, you should feel comfortable writing the simplest
possible app of all – which is a SharePoint hosted app. I
have some good news for you though, the REST and CSOM
API in SharePoint 2013 is so expansive and impressive that I
feel many business needs will be met via a simple SharePoint
hosted app. Apps can be quite capable. From here, we will
expand our apps horizon to,

a) Apps that need permissions to do specific things
b) Apps that use hosting environments other than SharePoint,
   a. Developer Hosted,
   b. Autohosted.

But, before continuing with all that, here is the section I promised you that will ensure you can actually run Apps on your environment. Yes I realize I should have presented this earlier in the book, but you should really go through my book at http://bit.ly/spdevmachine. I'll catch you with a further apps discussion in the "Client Webpart" section.

Configuring your development environment for Apps

There is one very important thing to know about apps and that is, when you install an app, a URL is created for you on the fly. A URL that looks like as below,

http://ws-05dfb3eee4cffa.apps.ws.int

The obvious question is how does this work on my dev. machine? More so, how will you set this up in production? The idea is, any URL that looks like this *.apps.ws.int, should resolve to an IP of your choice – the SharePoint server, in this case, the local dev box.

When you hit F5 from Visual Studio, Visual Studio sneakily edits your hosts file – pointing it to the local dev. machine. You never even notice it. But this won't work if you hand-deploy an app. In order for an on-the-fly created URL to work, here is how you need to setup your virtual machine development environment.

1. Add a new network card to your VM. Have this network card use a private network shared by the host, not use DHCP, and assign it a fixed IP address. I like to do this because my usual network card will keep changing its IP address as I move from hotel to client to airplanes. I would like my DNS settings to have some predictability in what IP they point to here, which is why you need a second network card. In production you will have a fixed IP anyway, so one network card is enough. I can't do that on my development machine because if I fixed the IP address on my main network card, internet will quit working on the VM and I would be unable to watch Lady Gaga videos on youtube when the app is deploying.

2. Then, open the DNS manager, and right click on "Forward lookup zones" and add a new zone called "apps.ws.int" with the following characteristics,
   a. Primary Zone,
   b. To all DNS servers running on in this domain: ws.int
   c. Zone name: apps.ws.int
   d. Do not allow dynamic updates

3. Next, in the DNS manager, right click on "apps.ws.int" and choose to add a new CNAME record, and enter

the details as below,

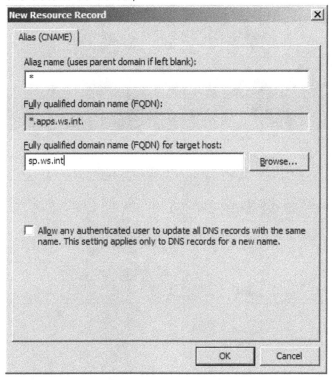

This will cause all requests to *.apps.ws.int to go to sp.ws.int.

To verify that requests are being routed properly, open command prompt and issue the following nslookup command,

```
C:\Windows\System32\drivers\etc>nslookup whateveryouwish.apps.ws.int
Server:  UnKnown
Address:  192.168.137.128

Name:     sp.ws.int
Addresses:  192.168.137.128
            192.168.137.128
Aliases:  whateveryouwish.apps.ws.int

C:\Windows\System32\drivers\etc>
```

Note that 192.168.137.128 is my machine's fixed IP address.

Also, verify that you can ping this as below,

```
C:\Windows\System32\drivers\etc>ping katyperry.apps.ws.int

Pinging sp.ws.int [192.168.137.128] with 32 bytes of data:
Reply from 192.168.137.128: bytes=32 time<1ms TTL=128
Reply from 192.168.137.128: bytes=32 time<1ms TTL=128
Reply from 192.168.137.128: bytes=32 time<1ms TTL=128
Reply from 192.168.137.128: bytes=32 time=1ms TTL=128

Ping statistics for 192.168.137.128:
    Packets: Sent = 4, Received = 4, Lost = 0 (0% loss),
Approximate round trip times in milli-seconds:
    Minimum = 0ms, Maximum = 1ms, Average = 0ms

C:\Windows\System32\drivers\etc>
```

As you can see, Katy Perry is responding to my pings. I really like her. I wish she was a better singer though.

Your final DNS setup should look like as below,

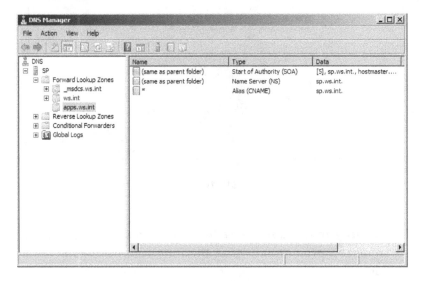

Your DNS is all setup but there is some more SharePoint setup to do. You need to configure the "app domain", which was that "apps.ws.int" suffix in the automatically provisioned DNS entry when you installed SharePoint. You will also have to configure the necessary service applications.

Configuring App Domain

As I mentioned earlier, to run app web, an app domain is required. It is very easy to create a new app domain and it can be created using either PowerShell or using the UI through central administration web application.

1. Launch SharePoint 2013 Management Shell (run as administrator) and run the following command.

   Oh and if it says "Set-SPAppDomain" is not a valid command, you probably didn't run SharePoint management shell as administrator.

2. Along with the app domain, you will also have to set App prefix text. This value will be used to build the app URL. To set the app prefix value using PowerShell, use the below script

```
Set-SPAppSiteSubscriptionName -Name "ws"-
Confirm:$false
```

   After the above command executes propely, output should return to prompt without any message as shown below.

```
PS C:\Users\administrator> Set-
SPAppSiteSubscriptionName -Name "ws" -site
"http://sp" -Confirm:$false
PS C:\Users\administrator>
```

3. From the central administration site, App domain can be set from the link Apps > Configure App URLS > App domain value. In the same screen, app prefix can be set as shown below.

Configure App URLs ⓘ

App URLs will be based on the following pattern: <app prefix> - <app id>.<app domain>

App domain

The app domain is the parent domain under which all apps will be hosted. You must already own this domain and have it configured in your DNS servers. It is recommended to use a unique domain for apps.

App domain:
apps.ws.int

App prefix

The app prefix will be prepended to the subdomain of the app URLs. Only letters and digits, no hyphens or periods allowed.

App prefix:
ws

Central Administration

Application Management
System Settings
Monitoring
Backup and Restore
Security
Upgrade and Migration
General Application Settings
Apps
Configuration Wizards

OK   Cancel

Once you set the URL's you will have to verify and set the service applications related to SharePoint apps.

Configuring Service Applications

There are two service applications that are required to run apps for SharePoint, **App Management Service** and **Microsoft SharePoint Foundation Subscription Settings Service**. If you have followed the steps in the "Setting up your SharePoint development environment" book, App Management Service would have been added and configured already. Microsoft SharePoint Foundation Subscription Settings Service is not available to install via the UI and hence it requires being added using PowerShell script.

1. Launch SharePoint 2013 Management Shell (run as administrator).
2. Get the service application for "App Management Service" or whatever name you used as below,

```
$sa = Get-SPServiceApplication | where-object { $_.displayname -eq "App Management Service" }
```

3. Create the subscription service as below,

```
$subsservice = New-
SPSubscriptionSettingsServiceApplication -
ApplicationPool $sa.ApplicationPool -Name
"Subscription Settings Service" -
DatabaseName "SubscriptionsDB"
```

4. Create proxy for the subscription service,

```
New-
SPSubscriptionSettingsServiceApplicationProx
y -ServiceApplication $subsservice
```

5. Start these services as below,

```
Get-SPServiceInstance | Where-Object {
$_.typename -eq "App Management Service" } |
Start-SPServiceInstance
Get-SPServiceInstance | Where-Object {
$_.typename -eq "Subscription Settings
Service" } | Start-SPServiceInstance
```

6. Once you have set the required service applications, you should be able to view the two service applications as shown below under Central Administration > System Settings > Manage Services on server. Ensure that these services are started.

7. To ensure that these service applications are associated with the web application, access the link

Central Administration > Application Management > Service Applications > Manage Service Applications and ensure that they are associated as shown in the figure below.

Once the required service applications are created and associated, configure apps for SharePoint.

The full powershell script is as below, but you do need to understand it before you blindly run it.

```
$sa = Get-SPServiceApplication | where-
object { $_.displayname -eq "App Management
Service" }
$subsservice = New-
SPSubscriptionSettingsServiceApplication -
ApplicationPool $sa.ApplicationPool -Name
"Subscription Settings Service" -
DatabaseName "SubscriptionsDB"
New-
SPSubscriptionSettingsServiceApplicationProx
y -ServiceApplication $subsservice
Get-SPServiceInstance | Where-Object {
$_.typename -eq "App Management Service" } |
Start-SPServiceInstance
Get-SPServiceInstance | Where-Object {
$_.typename -eq "Subscription Settings
Service" } | Start-SPServiceInstance
```

```
Set-SPAppDomain -appdomain "apps.ws.int"
Set-SPAppSiteSubscriptionName -Name "ws" -
Confirm:$false
```

Client Web Part

In the section of "writing your first app" you wrote the simple Appetizer. That app was quite nice, but it had one big problem – it ran full screen. In SharePoint, we are used to having multiple functional useful widgets on the same page – we call them WebParts.

The good news is, it is very easy to write an app that can work as a client WebPart

Begin Exercise: Appetizer Client WebPart

Assuming you have successfully authored the Appetizer, lets extend it to use a Client WebPart. To start with, ensure that you uninstall and remove Appetizer from both from http://sp and the app catalog so we have a clean environment to start with.

Next, in your Visual Studio 2012 appetizer project, choose to add a Client Web Part as shown below,

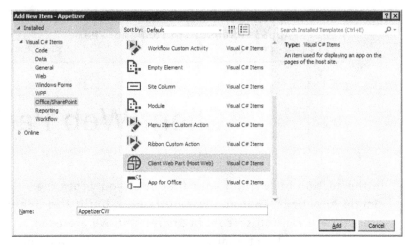

Choose to add a new client webpart page.

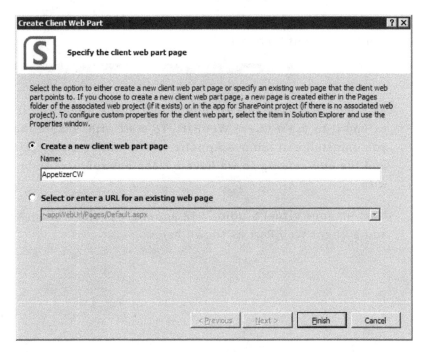

You do have the choice of picking the same Default.aspx also – but this presents an interesting UI challenge, you will see it soon. But for now, choose to add a new Client WebPart page. Notice that the page gets added to your Pages module as shown below,

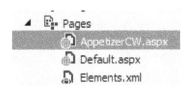

Next, in the Elements.xml of your newly added client
WebPart, add the following code,

```xml
<?xml version="1.0" encoding="utf-8"?>
<Elements xmlns="http://schemas.microsoft.com/sharepoint/">
  <ClientWebPart Name="AppetizerCW" Title="AppetizerCW Title" Description="AppetizerCW Description" DefaultWidth="300" DefaultHeight="200">
    <!-- Content element identifies the location of the page that will render inside the client web part
         Properties are referenced on the query string using the pattern _propertyName_
         Example: Src="~appWebUrl/Pages/ClientWebPart1.aspx?Property1=_property1_" -->
    <Content Type="html"
             Src="~appWebUrl/Pages/AppetizerCW.aspx?Property1=_prop1_&amp;Property2=_prop2_&amp;Property3=_prop3_&amp;Color=_color_" />
    <!-- Define properties in the Properties element.
         Remember to put Property Name on the Src attribute of the Content element above. -->
    <Properties>
      <Property
        Name="prop1"
        Type="string"
        WebBrowsable="true"
        WebDisplayName="First Property"
        WebDescription="Description 1"
        WebCategory="Custom Properties"
        DefaultValue="String Property"
        RequiresDesignerPermission="true" />
      <Property
        Name="prop2"
        Type="boolean"
        WebBrowsable="true"
        WebDisplayName="Second Property"
        WebDescription="Description 2"
        WebCategory="Custom Properties"
        DefaultValue="TRUE"
        RequiresDesignerPermission="true" />
      <Property
        Name="prop3"
        Type="int"
        WebBrowsable="true"
        WebDisplayName="Third Property"
        WebDescription="Description 3"
        WebCategory="Custom Properties"
        DefaultValue="1"
        RequiresDesignerPermission="true" />
      <Property
        Name="color"
        Type="enum"
        WebBrowsable="true"
        WebDisplayName="Fourth Property"
        WebDescription="Sets color for the CW"
        WebCategory="Custom Properties"
        DefaultValue="blue"
        RequiresDesignerPermission="true" >
        <EnumItems>
          <EnumItem Value="blue" WebDisplayName="Blue" />
          <EnumItem Value="red" WebDisplayName="Red" />
          <EnumItem Value="yellow" WebDisplayName="Yellow" />
        </EnumItems>
      </Property>
    </Properties>
  </ClientWebPart>
</Elements>
```

The above sppipet uses a special CAML element called
"ClientWebPart" – this is new in SharePoint 2013.

Next open the AppetizerCW.aspx and add a reference to
jQuery

```
<script type="text/javascript" src="../Scripts/jquery-1.7.1.min.js"></script>
```

And add the following JavaScript method,

```
function getParameterByName(name) {
    var match = RegExp('[?&]' + name + '=([^&]*)')
                    .exec(window.location.search);
    return match && decodeURIComponent(match[1].replace(/\+/g, ' '));
}
```

Finally, in the body tag, add the following code,

```
<body style="width:100%;text-align:center">
    <br /><input type="button" onclick="$('body').css('background-color', getParameterByName('Color'));" value="Change Color"/>
</body>
```

Finally, in App.js, in the onGetUserNameSuccess, add the following code,

```
// Show Query string parameters
var vars = [], hash;
var q = document.URL.split('?')[1];
if (q != undefined) {
    q = q.split('&');
    for (var i = 0; i < q.length; i++) {
        hash = q[i].split('=');
        vars.push(hash[1]);
        vars[hash[0]] = hash[1];
        $('#message').append("<br/><b>" + decodeURIComponent(hash[0]) + "</b>: " + decodeURIComponent(hash[1]));
    }
}
```

The above code prints out all querystring parameters passed in.

Press F5 to deploy your app, verify that the app prints out an output similar to the below,

Hello Administrator
SPHostUrl: http://sp
SPLanguage: en-US
SPClientTag: 0
SPProductNumber: 15.0.4420.1017
SPAppWebUrl: http://ws-d21e0710089a91.apps.ws.int/Appetizer

But hitting F5 would run the App in full screen, we are interested in seeing it run as a WebPart (or client WebPart to be more exact). While the app is still running, go to http://sp, and put it's home page in edit mode. Delete all webparts from the home page, and choose to add a WebPart, note that there is also a link called "App Part" compare what you see in AppPart vs. WebPart, what do you see?

Next, see the Apps section? Add your App on the page,

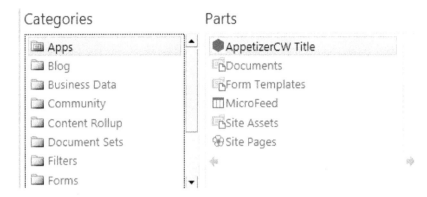

Click on the "Change color" button to verify that the color of the webpart changes as shown below,

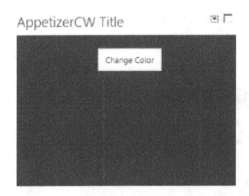

Next, edit this webpart, and set the following values,

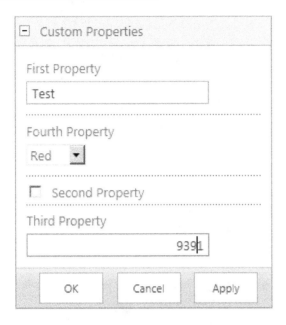

And click ok .. click on "Change Color" one more time to verify that the color looks as below,

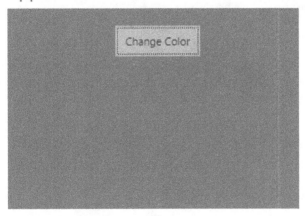

Next, stop debugging, and open the elements.xml for your AppetizerCW.aspx, and change the following line ..

```
<Content Type="html"
    Src="~appWebUrl/Pages/AppetizerCW.aspx?Property1=_prop1_&amp;Property2=_prop2_&amp;Property3=_prop3_&amp;Color=_color_" />
```

To ..

```
<Content Type="html"
    Src="~appWebUrl/Pages/Default.aspx?Property1=_prop1_&amp;Property2=_prop2_&amp;Property3=_prop3_&amp;Color=_color_" />
```

Press F5 to deploy your app 1 more time. Once the app is deployed, go back to http://sp. And verify that your page looks like as shown below,

Huh? Why is this not working? The answer is, by default the page is prevented from running in an IFRAME, there is a very good reason for this. Running in an IFRAME means the outside page has full access to what is inside. This means, an unscrupulous user can hit F12 and well, access anything in your JS DOM.

POTHOLE ALERT: Avoid mixing the following three together,

a) An App that accesses any third party secure data that you don't feel comfortable sharing with the user or any code running on the host page.
b) The app running as a client WebPart
c) The secure code written purely on client side

Why? Because imagine if you had an App that allowed you to transfer money from one bank account into another, it would do so via OAuth (usually) for which it will need to get an access token so it can do such actions using your permissions. What prevents an outside sandbox solution on the host page showing funny cat videos from getting a hold of this access token and doing balance transfers from your account into mine? Answer: Nothing! Ouch!

Anyway, back to our app, the default.aspx won't load huh? Stop debugging, add the following in default.aspx and try again,

<WebPartPages:AllowFraming runat="server" />

Verify that you are able to see the below,

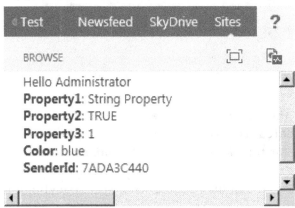

There is one big issue I see above – those ugly scrollbars. Can I somehow write an app that works both in full screen experience and as a client WebPart and still look nice? The answer? Easy! Just write the logic of your app as an ASCX, and embed it on two pages – one that acts as the client WebPart, second that acts as the full screen app. Later on you will see that the branding and look and feel is due to the chrome control – and you can choose to not load it programmatically as well. Problem solved.

UI Custom Action App

Yet another way to launch apps is via a custom action. The idea here is that you can use the CustomAction element and provide a launching mechanism for a full screen app. Let's see this in action.

In your Appetizer project, choose to add a Menu Item custom action as shown below,

Choose to target the action as shown below,

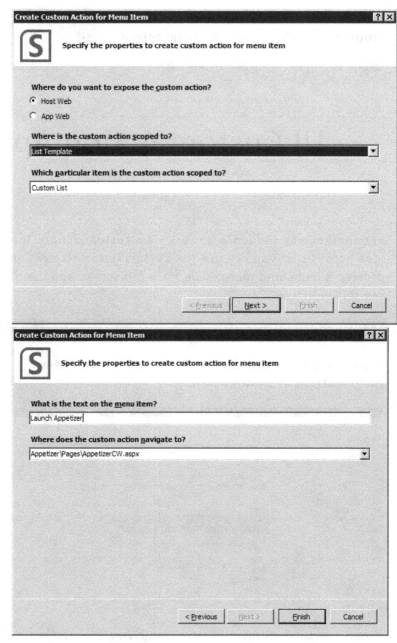

Go ahead and deploy your app, once the app is deployed, go to the host web, create a list based on the custom list template and add a list item in it.

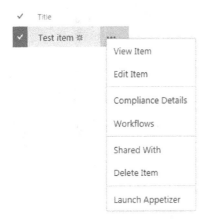

Verify that clicking on the "Launch Appetizer" link launches the app in the browser window.

Now, stop debugging, and add the following three attributes in the Elements.xml in the AppetizerCustomAction as shown below,

```xml
<?xml version="1.0" encoding="utf-8"?>
<Elements xmlns="http://schemas.microsoft.com/sharepoint/">
  <CustomAction Id="e794bdc4-01eb-49e0-9206-86c3df714d17.AppetizerCustomAction"
                RegistrationType="List"
                RegistrationId="100"
                Location="EditControlBlock"
                Sequence="10001"
                Title="Launch Appetizer"
                HostWebDialog="TRUE"
                HostWebDialogHeight="500"
                HostWebDialogWidth="500"
                >
  <!--
```

Go ahead and deploy the app one more time, and launch it just like before on the custom list item, verify that you are able to run the app, but this time it launches in a dialog as shown below,

End Exercise: Appetizer Custom Action

Congratulations, pat yourself on the back, you're already an expert at writing SharePoint hosted apps. What's left to do? Well introduce the server side story – writing server side apps. The thing though is, not just yet! There is an interesting new thing we need to keep our eyes on, which is, writing an App, using an App, that is NAPA!

NAPA Development Tools

Apps can be really powerful. In fact, to prove that, the Visual Studio team at Microsoft wrote an App, that lets you write Apps. This is right now called Codename NAPA Development tools. Now, don't uninstall Visual Studio just yet. There is a lot that Visual Studio has that NAPA doesn't. Such as integrating with source control, unit testing, working together as a team, and a lot lot LOT more.

But, sometimes you don't have Visual Studio, or imagine a small mom and pop shop that gets Office 365, they are willing to write some simple code and author an app, but don't have Visual Studio. In those instances, NAPA will really help you out. Without much further ado, lets get familiarized with NAPA before we jump into provider hosted apps.

Begin Exercise: NAPA Dev tools

Before you start this exercise let me say a couple of things,

a) NAPA is not production ready – I wouldn't uninstall Visual Studio just yet.
b) NAPA is a moving target, it is changing rapidly, so look at this exercise as "understand the concepts" some of the screenshots may be different than what you see.
c) It is good to learn about NAPA for 2 reasons
   a. It might get you out of a bind when you don't have Visual Studio
   b. There is a very good chance that this will grow into something important in the future.

In the current incarnation of NAPA, to get started, you need to go to dev.office.com. When this site is launched, it would look like as below,

Build apps for Office and SharePoint

Embracing web standards, the new cloud app model gives you maximum choice and flexibility to build a new class of apps for Office and SharePoint using familiar languages, tools, and hosting services. Visit the Explore section to learn more and start creating your own apps that will soon be in the hands of millions of people.

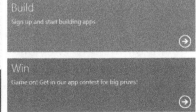

Click on the "Build" button, you will have to go through a sign up process at this time. If you have already signed up for Office365, click on the sign in button on the top right hand corner. Note that the SharePoint developer site may not be available immediately. You can check the status of the developer site by signing in at https://portal.microsoftonline.com/admin/default.aspx and checking the status as shown below,

Welcome to Office 365 Preview Developer Pack Preview!
Build apps on the developer site (wait for SharePoint to be provisioned...)

Once on the developer site, it should look like as below,

✎ EDIT LINKS

Developer Site

Get started with Office Apps   REMOVE THIS

Get tools to build apps

Publish to Office Store

Learn to use the developer site

Now, it may be tempting to click on the "Get tools to build apps" button, but stop! The tools are installed as an app. So first, at the bare minimum, you need to setup the app catalog. In order to do so, when logged into your Office 365 dashboard, look at the top right hand corner, and click on the Admin link and go to SharePoint admin. Then, in the menu on the left, click on "Apps" and create a new app catalog. I created mine at /sites/appcat. This may take a few seconds to provision, so be patient. You can monitor the progress on the SharePoint administration center.

Once you have setup apps, go to the developer site once more, and Click on the "Get tools to build apps" button, You will then be taken to a page that will allow you to install the NAPA development tools for free. Click on the "Add it" button. Now at this point you may be asked to login to your Microsoft account. Like a dumbdonkey, I kept entering my Office 365 account here. What they mean here is, enter your live id — but since the "live" branding is being discontinued, they call it Microsoft account, not the "onmicrosoft" account. Argh!

Anyway, the "onmicrosoft" account vs. the Microsoft account issue makes sense if you consider that the app belongs to you, not to your SharePoint site.

Once you have added the app, you should be able to see the app added in your site contents page as shown below,

✎ EDIT LINKS

Site Contents

Lists, Libraries, and other Apps

add an app

"Napa" Office 365 Development Tools

new!

Form Templates
0 items
Modified 2 months ago

Nintex Workflow Platform Preview

new!

Go ahead and click on the Purple icon that says "Napa" office 365 development tools. You would be redirected to www.napacloudapp.com. Here, you are presented with various kinds of apps you can create. I am going to create a fancy SharePoint app as shown below,

Soon as the app is created, you immediately notice a few interesting things.

1. You get code highlighting, just like Visual Studio.
2. You even get intellisense. Not only that you get JavaScript intellisense and statement completion that is smart enough to understand what JavaScript functions are in scope.

```
12  function sharePointReady() {
13      context = new SP.ClientContext.get_current();
14      web = context.get_web();
15      get
16          🛈 get
17  }       🛈 get_current
18          🛈 get_currentUser
19  // T    🛈 get_message
20  func    🛈 get_title
21          🛈 get_web
22          🛈 getUserName
23
24  }
25
```

This is pretty amazing because it is constantly checking the structure of your would-be page and sort of performing a pseudo compilation of your page.

3. You have a "solution explorer" and you can even upload new files or rename/delete existing files.

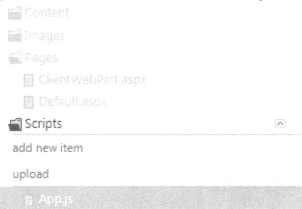

4. And at the very bottom, you see a toolbar

The last icon is interesting – "Open in Visual Studio". As you play with Napa, you will find that frequently you will run into a wall as far as the capabilities of Napa is concerned. One big limitation is lack of source control, which for development projects is absolutely essential. Therefore, Microsoft gives us the ability to export this project into Visual Studio, where a quick painless installation will lead you to a thick client development experience, wired to Office 365. No longer do you have to deal with the hassles of creating a big development rig.

Anyway, let's finish our Napa app. What I wanted to do was to impress my friends with an app that would show funny cat pictures from Flickr. What I found out was that there is a flickr api that I can call at http://api.flickr.com/services/feeds/photos_public.gne and pass it the necessary parameters to get cat pictures as a JSON feed. This will be a cross-domain JSON request so there are some intricacies to solve, but nothing that is out of our reach.

The first thing I need is jQuery, so I can use methods such as $.getJSON. The NAPA SharePoint project template already has a reference to jQuery 1.6.2, I don't like that reference for two reasons,

1. It is jQuery 1.6.2, so outdated.
2. It will not auto-update when newer versions of jQuery are available.

So, I went ahead and changed that reference to,

```
http://code.jquery.com/jquery-latest.js
```

Next, I changed the "PlaceHolderMain" content place holder to as follows,

```
<asp:Content
ContentPlaceHolderId="PlaceHolderMain"
runat="server">
        <div id="catimages">
                Standby .. loading cats ..
        </div>
</asp:Content>
```

As you can see, I have a single div here that is going to show cat images. So far so good! Next, I went ahead and edited the app.js to as shown below,

```
var context;
var web;
var user;

// This code runs when the DOM is ready. It
ensures the SharePoint
// script file sp.js is loaded and then
executes sharePointReady()
$(document).ready(function () {
    SP.SOD.executeFunc('sp.js',
'SP.ClientContext', sharePointReady);
```

```
});

// This function creates a context object
which is needed to use the SharePoint object
model
function sharePointReady() {
        $.getJSON("http://api.flickr.com/servi
ces/feeds/photos_public.gne?jsoncallback=?",
        {
                tags: "silly cat",
                tagmode: "any",
                format: "json"
        },
                function(data) {
                $("#catimages").html("");
                $.each(data.items,
function(i,item){
                        $("<img/>").attr("src",
item.media.m).appendTo("#catimages");
                                if ( i === 3 ) return
false;
                });
        });
}
```

As you can see, NAPA is quite smart when it comes to enforcing good JavaScript. You will note that I have a "===" which is good practice in JavaScript since it does a type safe equality comparison. Change that to "==" and Napa will give you an appropriate warning.

Also, one of the biggest issues in writing JavaScript is matching all those parenthesis, and curly braces. Napa also shows you matching braces as you are editing code.

Our app is now complete. Hit the "play" button in the toolbar at the very bottom. You will note that Napa will build and install your app, and launch SharePoint with your app installed. You will need to allow popups for SharePoint to launch.

Package   Deploy   Launch

Uploading

Your project is being packaged and installed on your
SharePoint server.

Cancel

And soon as the application launches, you should see your
first app in it's full glory,

Napa will also let you tweak this project further, and even
enable you to talk to SharePoint via its permissioning model.
You can tweak permissions by going to properties for the
Napa app, and going to the properties tab as shown below,

Properties

General	∧ Content				Set the permissions which will cause your app for SharePoint to request from the user at installation time.
Client Web Part	Tenant		None		
Permissions	Site Collection		None		
Remote Endpoints	Web		None		
	List		None		
	∧ Services				
	BCS		None		
	Search		None		
	Taxonomy		None		
	∨ Social				
	∨ Project				

There are other kinds of apps that you can write with Napa as well. I leave it up to you to explore that.

Now that I have written such a productive and useful app, I wish to source control it, and possibly distribute it on the open app store. In order to do so, I simply click on the "Launch in Visual studio" button, which prompts me to download an exe as shown below,

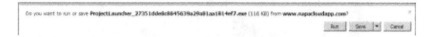

I go ahead and run the EXE, and Visual Studio 2012 launches with the project opened up nicely. In this project, there are a few things to notice,

a) This project is running in Visual Studio, all files are local, but they are connected to the cloud equivalents. Just go ahead and open any file, and Visual Studio will prompt you to login with your SharePoint credentials. Here on, Visual studio will keep everything in sync both on your local machine, in your source control, and in the cloud.

b) The site url property of this project is pointing to the online cloud hosted Office 365 site. This allows you to write apps, without a big SharePoint installation locally installed.

c) You can easily right click the app, and choose to publish it. This will give you a .app file that you can submit to the SharePoint store, or distribute it within your organization.

Now, you can take that .app file and submit it to the open SharePoint app store. I tried to get my funny cat pictures app published, but Microsoft rejected it. I have no idea why since it is such a useful app.

End Exercise: NAPA Dev tools

Great! So far, we have covered a pretty good expanse around apps that run 100% in SharePoint. There is a HostWeb, there is an AppWeb, but they are both in the same SharePoint installation. You may be wondering why should I ever bother to write a SharePoint hosted app? Isn't a sandbox solution equally powerful, or perhaps more powerful because it can do server side code?

The one line answer is – sandbox code doesn't understand the concept of App Permissions.

Lets understand App Permissions.

App Permissions

Wouldn't it be nice if there were no thieves? I would never have to worry about locking my house, my car, we would have no passwords, no reason to authenticate.

Time to wake up! The internet is what I think of as a medium sized city. It is still nascent if you think about it – it has been around for maybe 10 or 15 years in its commercial form. And we already entrust the internet with millions or even billions of dollars' worth of ecommerce.

Frankly makes me nervous, but not like there are many alternatives. Like any growing city, the thieves are becoming braver and more cunning. On the other hand, the need for complex applications that need to do so much is also increasing.

Apps, you can also imagine, are going to need to do more than say "Hello World". Sometimes these apps will need access to parts of SharePoint that should require the user's "okay". These permissions are by definition are also supposed to work in a cross-domain model, especially where authentication is done using client side redirects, REST API, over HTTPs etc.

This isn't a new challenge however. If you have a Facebook account, you might have used your Facebook identity to leave a comment on a website. Facebook will ask you if the website is allowed to gain certain permissions, such as post to your profile. All that is built on a technology called OAuth. OAuth is what SharePoint uses also for app's security and permissions.

Security in SharePoint is more than just OAuth though. There are concepts of cross-domain security etc. that we need to be familiar with as well.

I view learning about SharePoint App security in two main buckets,

a) How client side code works in cross-domain requests.
b) How server side code works in cross-domain requests.

Both of the above work in completely different ways – they are both described later in the book. But, both can request permissions.

Whenever an app is installed in SharePoint, it requests for permissions it needs during installation from the user installing the app. The developer of the app must specify ahead of time what permissions the app needs. The user installing the app is the one who grants the requested permissions – as a rule, the user himself must have the permission they are granting. There are some exceptions to this rule such as App only permissions policy (described later) and on-the-fly permissions (also described later).

There are some key points to consider here,

1. The developer specifies what permissions an app will require
2. The developer can only request the kind of permission, such as "read access to web", the developer cannot specify site specific artifacts in the permissions, such as "read access to a specific SPWeb". This makes sense because the apps could end up on an app store and details of where the app will be installed should be agnostic to the app. The exception to this rule is when requesting permissions to lists where you can ask for access to a specific list types. But you still cannot request for permission to a specific list. In fact, your app must not know or rely upon the presence of a list.
   a. **POTHOLE ALERT**: Sounds great! Except to discover the list of lists in your HostWeb, you need to ask for FullControl. That wouldn't be so bad except once you grant such a permission the app can do anything as long as it stays under that permission. This becomes an issue in provider hosted apps, where you gave the app permissions to write to the "current weather list", but lets say the provider hosted app server gets hacked, they can write to your announcements list now. What worries me especially is that every app, even if you don't ask for any permissions, has

www.winsmarts.com | 75 | Page

some basic permissions to the SPWeb, which includes "basic user permission". Sounds like a great way for a budding vendor to steal the names of users in a SharePoint site and use them as sales leads.

3. The user installing the app grants the permissions. The user granting the permissions cannot grant the app any permission that the user himself doesn't have. App only permission policy apps must be installed by site collection administrators.
4. The user can grant all or none of the permissions – the user cannot pick and choose what permissions to grant.
5. If the user denies permissions, the app is not installed.

Whenever you build an app, it is comprised of some basic identifying information, the AppID (sometimes called as ClientID), Display Name, App URI and optionally a redirect URI for on the fly permissions. These are required bits of information whether the app is being trusted via ACS or is being installed as a high-trust app on-premises.

The app developer specifies the permissions required as the permission level required on a certain scope.

The scopes available are,

Scope	URI	Permission levels available
SPSite	http://sharepoint/content/sitecollection/	Read, Write, Manage, FullControl are available
SPWeb	http://sharepoint/content/sitecollection/web	Read, Write, Manage, FullControl are

		available
SPList	http://sharepoint/content/sitecollection/web/list	Read, Write, Manage, FullControl are available
Tenancy	http://<sharepointserver>/<content>/<tenant>/	Read, Write, Manage, FullControl are available
BCS	http://sharepoint/bcs/connection	Read
Search	http://sharepoint/search	QueryAsUserIgnoreAppPrincipal
Project Server	http://sharepoint/projectserver	Manage
Project Server	http://sharepoint/projectserver/projects	Read, Write
Project Server	http://sharepoint/projectserver/projects/project	Read, Write
Project Server	http://sharepoint/projectserver/enterpriseresources	Read, Write

Proje ct Serve r	http://sharepoint/projectserver/statusing	SubmitStatus
Proje ct Serve r	http://sharepoint/projectserver/reporting	Read
Proje ct Serve r	http://sharepoint/projectserver/workflow	Elevate
Social	http://sharepoint/social/tenant	Read, Write, Manage, FullControl
Social	http://sharepoint/social/core	Read, Write, Manage, FullControl
Social	http://sharepoint/social/microfeed	Read, Write, Manage, FullControl
Taxon omy	http://sharepoint/taxonomy	Read, Write

It is worth pointing out that not all of the above permissions apply to every SKU. And there is a possibility that with future products you may see additional permission levels added.

Note that in requesting a scope you specific a generic URL – you cannot specify a real URL of a real list for instance. In other words, http://sp/lists/customerslist is not a valid scope. This is done on purpose since apps will be available in the appstore, they will be installed across many sites, and they must not rely site specific artifacts. That http://sharepoint you see in the table above is not a real URL.

You may however request permissions to a certain kind of list based on List Template ID as shown below,

```
<AppPermissionRequest
Scope="http://sharepoint/content/sitecollect
ion/web/list" Right="Write">
    <Property Name="BaseTemplateId"
Value="101"/>
</AppPermissionRequest>
```

Also, generally speaking, when a permission is granted on a parent, the app automatically gets permissions to all the children. Permissions in fact are almost exactly like the permissions you grant to users. The permission levels are also quite identical. When an app is installed, an Appprincipal is created – this is not a user that you can add into a SharePoint securable object. But it is there, you can find it using the object model.

The big difference between permission levels granted to users, and the permission levels granted to app principals is that the permission levels granted to app principals are not customizable. What I mean by this is, "Manage" permission level on every environment for Apps will be exactly the same – this is not something you can customize. This is a good thing because an app written for on-premises will continue to run in the cloud, your app does not need to consider platform centric eccentricities. Also as a part of standard tokens you do get the SP Build version, so your app can accommodate for future changes in apps.

The app requests permissions on a scope – and can request any of the following level of permission,

Permission Request	Description	Permissions included	Other Notes
Read	Enables apps to view pages, list items, and download documents.	• View Items • Open Items • View Versions • Create Alerts • Use Self-Service Site Creation • View Pages	
Write	Enables apps to view, add, update, and delete items in existing lists and document libraries.	• Read-Only permissions, plus: • Add Items • Edit Items • Delete Items • Delete Versions • Browse Directories • Edit Personal User Information • Manage Personal Views	

		• Add/Remove Personal Web Parts	
		• Update Personal Web Parts	
Manage	Enables apps to view, add, update, delete, approve, and customize items or pages within a web site.	• Write permissions, plus: • Manage Lists • Add and Customize Pages • Apply Themes and Borders • Apply Style Sheets	Not available to taxonomy
Full Control	Enables apps to have full control within the specified scope.	• All permissions	Not available to Office store apps. If you try and submit an app that requests full control to the office store, it is blocked. Such an app can

			however can still be installed via app catalog.
Query	Enables apps to issue search queries	• Search	Available for search only
SubmitStat us and Elevate	Project Server only	• SubmitStat us and Elevate	SubmitStat us and Elevate

App authorization policies

In addition to determining the app permission request scope and the app permission request level for each app you deploy, you must also determine which app authorization policy is appropriate. SharePoint 2013 provides the following app authorization policies:

- **User-only policy**— This is what we usually think of code running in SharePoint. This means, the code is running as the user running it – and code is able to access a resource if the logged in user has access to the resource. An example of when this policy is enforced is when the user is accessing resources directly without using the app. Here the SAML token is examined and your code can do stuff.

- **User + app policy**— This is new in SharePoint 2013. With this policy, the authorization checks take into account both the user identity and the app identity. In particular, when this policy is used, authorization checks succeed only if <u>both</u> the current user and the app have sufficient permissions to perform the action in question. This is usually the most common scenario when it comes to Apps.

- **App-only policy**— This is also new in SharePoint 2013. With this policy, authorization checks take into account only the app identity. In particular, when this policy is used, an authorization check succeeds only if the current app has sufficient permissions to perform the action in question, regardless of the permissions of the current user (if any). This can also be thought of as "elevation" or in scenarios where he user identity is not available such as anonymous scenarios (think WCM sites). Also, in order to grant permissions to such an App, you have to be a site collection administrator. In the app-only policy app type, the person who installs the app (for example, a human resources manager) has the rights that the app needs, *even though users who actually use the app might not have those rights*.

In order to use the App only policy, you need the following XML snippet in your AppManifest.xml

```
<AppPermissionRequests
AllowAppOnlyPolicy="true">
```

There are a few things you need to know about AllowAppOnlyPolicy though,

1. Not all APIs support App-Only policy, notably the search and project server APIs do not allow this.
2. A user must be a site collection administrator to be able to grant use of the app-only policy. If the app-only policy is granted and the app already has

tenant-scoped permissions, then the user must be a tenant administrator to be able to grant use of the app-only policy.

3. At runtime, apps opt into using the app-only policy by making a request with which they pass an app-only token. The following code example shows how an app can get an app-only access token in Azure ACS/OAuth apps (note the below code goes in the server side area of provider hosted apps – which I haven't talked about yet):

```
string appOnlyAccessToken =
TokenHelper.GetAppOnlyAccessToken(contextTok
en.TargetPrincipalName,
sharepointUrl.Authority,
contextToken.Realm).AccessToken;
```

4. Only apps with web applications running outside of SharePoint can create and pass app-only tokens. In other words, SharePoint hosted apps do not use App only authorization policy. This is a very good thing, can you guess why? Because if JavaScript could use App only policies, anyone could hack the DOM and elevate themselves to the Apps permission. I'm glad we can't do that.

5. In the case of app-only policy, SharePoint creates a SHAREPOINT\APP, similar to the existing SHAREPOINT\SYSTEM user. All app-only requests are made by SHAREPOINT\APP.

This brings me to an important point about App-Only policies which might be getting obvious to those of you whose left eyebrow is raised. App-Only policies can be thought of as "Elevation". You need to be careful who you grant this right to. Remember, after you have trusted the app, nothing prevents the app author from changing the server side code and abuse that elevation you have trusted them with. As a golden rule, when drawling a circle around the servers you need to protect and secure, the App server (the server on which server side code for apps runs), must be inside that circle.

NOTE: Apps can also be managed by administrators using PowerShell. For a list of App Management Service cmdlets in SharePoint 2013, please see the following link. http://technet.microsoft.com/en-us/library/jj219772(v=office.15).aspx

Requesting Permissions – the AppManifest.xml

Okay so with all this basic theory behind us, you might be wondering, how you the developer can specify that your app needs a certain set of permissions? The answer is, you specify this by editing the AppManifest.xml. Here is an example,

```
<?xml version="1.0" encoding="utf-8" ?>
<App xmlns=http://schemas.microsoft.com/sharepoint/2012/app/manifest
.. other stuff ..
>
.. other stuff ..
<AppPermissionRequests>
<AppPermissionRequest Scope="http://sharepoint/content/sitecollection/web" Right="Read" />
</AppPermissionRequests>
</App>
```

That's really how simple it is. The above code snippet will request "read" access to the SPWeb. The exception to this rule is On-The-Fly permissions where a webpage or app can request for certain permissions on-demand at runtime, not during install time. Those permissions are good only for a limited duration. I describe this later in the book.

Cross Domain Security – Client Side Only

I'm glad you're an expert on App Permissions now, because with this background, I can talk about a very interesting topic, which is cross domain security. Apps run on a separate URL. Server side code authenticates using OAuth or S2S, but client side code uses a different approach.

What happens is,

a) When your app loads, it is passed in the SPHostURL. This is usually included in the {StandardTokens} querystring app replacement token. For this {StandardTokens} to work, unfortunately you need to have a real AppWeb, which means your app needs to have a dummy feature in it – even if it doesn't do anything. Yuck, icky! But, it is what it is. For more details, please see the section "App replacement tokens" section further in the book.

b) Anyway, so your app has the SPHostURL, using which it loads the http://(sphosturl)/_layouts/15/SP.RequestExecutor.js file.

c) Additionally, your app will contain an http://(appWebUrl)/_layouts/15/AppWebProxy.aspx URL in an IFRAME on the same page.

d) So what happens now is that, anytime you wish to make a call to the hostweb – and this applies to both CSOM and REST API, your request is actually made to the AppWebProxy, which then funnels that request to the server side.

e) The server recognizes that request coming from a registered app, and it allows the request to be executed under the apps granted permissions.

f) Data is returned back to the IFRAME which is then returned back to your script.

The best part, all this is actually a whole lot simpler for you when you actually write this code. Lets see an example.

BEGIN EXERCISE: Cross Domain REST Call

In this exercise, I will write a simple app that executes a cross domain REST call. Start by creating a Provider hosted SharePoint 2013 app called CrossDomainREST. Now why am I creating a provider hosted app? Especially that I haven't yet talked about provider hosted apps.

Simple! I want to emphasize that this indeed works cross domain. We will get rid of any server side code for the provider hosted app though.

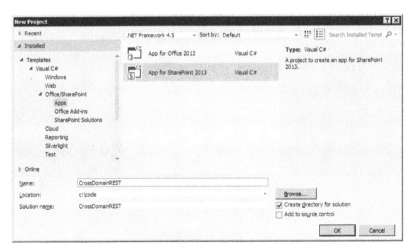

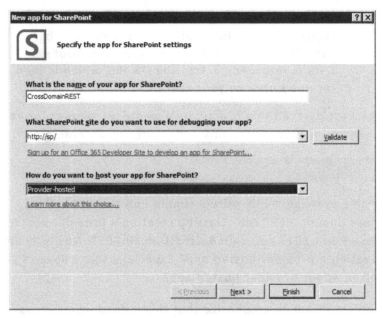

Once the app gets created, we need to do some cleanup. The clean up is for one reason – that we wish to demonstrate that everything here can be done in pure JavaScript. We are not concerned about server side code just yet.

Delete the Pages folder and the TokenHelper.cs files

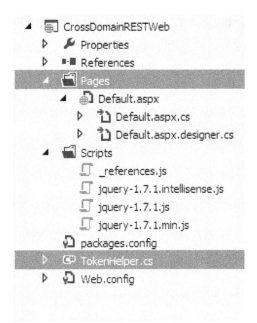

Next, add two files – REST.html and REST.js, your project should look like as below,

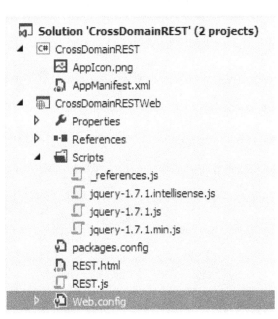

Double click on AppManifest.xml, and change the Start Page: to CrossDomainRESTWeb/REST.html

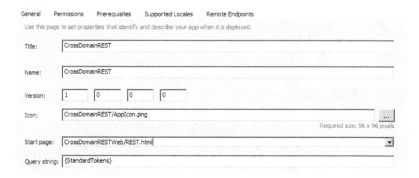

In the REST.html file, add the following code,

```
<!DOCTYPE html>
<html>
    <head>
        <title>Cross-domain REST</title>
        <script src="http://ajax.aspnetcdn.com/ajax/4.0/1/MicrosoftAjax.js" type="text/javascript"></script>
        <script type="text/javascript" src="../Scripts/jquery-1.7.1.min.js"></script>
        <script type="text/javascript" src="REST.js"></script>
    </head>
    <body>
        <div id="listsList"></div>
    </body>
</html>
```

And in REST.js, add the following code,

```
var hostweburl;
var appweburl;

$(document).ready(function () {
    hostweburl = decodeURIComponent(getQueryStringParameter("SPHostUrl"));
    appweburl = decodeURIComponent(getQueryStringParameter("SPAppWebUrl"));
    var scriptbase = hostweburl + "/_layouts/15/";
    $.getScript(scriptbase + "SP.RequestExecutor.js", execCrossDomainRequest);
});

function execCrossDomainRequest() {
    var executor = new SP.RequestExecutor(appweburl);
    executor.executeAsync(
        {
            url: appweburl + "/_api/web/lists",
            method: "GET",
            headers: { "Accept": "application/json; odata=verbose" },
            success: function (data) {
                var jsonObject = JSON.parse(data.body);
                var htmlText = "";
                var results = jsonObject.d.results;
                for (var i = 0; i < results.length; i++) {
                    htmlText = htmlText + "<p><h1>" + results[i].Title + "<h1></p>";
                }
                document.getElementById("listsList").innerHTML = htmlText;
            },
            error: function (data, errorCode, errorMessage) {
                document.getElementById("listsList").innerText =
                    "Could not complete cross-domain call: " + errorMessage;
            }
        }
    );
}

function getParameterByName(name) {
    var match = RegExp('[?&]' + name + '=([^&]*)')
                    .exec(window.location.search);
    return match && decodeURIComponent(match[1].replace(/\+/g, ' '));
}

function getQueryStringParameter(paramToRetrieve) {
    var params =
        document.URL.split("?")[1].split("&");
    var strParams = "";
    for (var i = 0; i < params.length; i = i + 1) {
        var singleParam = params[i].split("=");
        if (singleParam[0] == paramToRetrieve)
            return singleParam[1];
    }
}
```

What we are doing here is, when the page loads, we execute
"execCrossDomainRequest". And in this we execute a REST
call to get /_api/web/lists. Note that this will be a cross
domain request. The URL is appWebURL/* but we are trying
to get the list of lists from the hostweb.

What is most important however is that you are executing your REST calls through **SP.RequestExecutor.** This basically sends your calls via AppWebProxy.

On success we simply write out the list of lists fetched.

Now we need to do something strange. Apps have an issue where SharePoint won't send the querystring parameters in the app, unless the app has an AppWeb. So, go ahead and add a feature/package in it. You can do this easily by adding an empty element in the CrossDomainREST project as shown below,

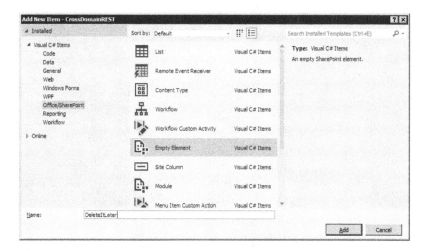

Once you have created this empty element, delete it, and delete the associated feature, but don't delete the package. Your project should look like as below,

Next, select the CrossDomainRESTWeb project and in it's properties, change SSL Enabled to "False".

Press F5 to deploy the and run the app. You may get the below dialog, just hit "Yes" – usually you get this for provider hosted apps – visual studio is setting up everything for us behind the scenes. For now, we don't need this portion – we will dive deeper into this when we talk about provider hosted apps, but just hit OK for now.

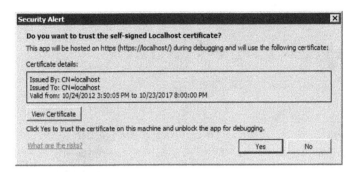

Go ahead and trust the app,

Do you trust CrossDomainREST?

Let it access basic information about this site.

Let it access basic information about the users of this site.

CrossDomainREST

Trust It   Cancel

Verify that you are able to run the app as shown below,

Composed Looks

Master Page Gallery

Functional, but wow what an ugly app. Where did all my nice SharePoint branding go? That is a job for something called as "Chrome Control" – I will cover that next when I talk about CSOM Cross Domain calls.

There is no branding here because we haven't integrated the chrome control – we shall do that in the next lab. But, open IE dev toolbar by hitting F12, and examine the structure of the HTML as shown below,

```
<!DOCTYPE html>
<html>
  <head>
    Text - Empty Text Node
    <title>
    Text - Empty Text Node
    <script src="http://ajax.aspnetcdn.com/ajax/4.0/1/MicrosoftAjax.js" type="text/javascript"></scrip
    Text - Empty Text Node
    <script src="../Scripts/jquery-1.7.1.min.js" type="text/javascript"></script>
    Text - Empty Text Node
    <script src="REST.js" type="text/javascript"></script>
    Text - Empty Text Node
  <body>
    Text - Empty Text Node
    <div id="listsList">
    Text - Empty Text Node
    <iframe id="http://ws-d21e0710089a9a.apps.ws.int/crossdomainrest/_layouts/15/AppWebProxy.aspx" src
```

Note that there is an IFrame that loads

http://ws-d21e0710089a9a.apps.ws.int/crossdomainrest/_layouts/15/AppWebProxy.aspx.

Also you can run Fiddler and verify that you are loading SP.RequestExecutor.js from the host web.

	8	200	HTTP	sp	/_layouts/15/SP.RequestExecutor.js?_=1350201288709
	10	401	HTTP	ws-05dfb2c6186e4...	/crossdomainapprest/_layouts/15/AppWebProxy.aspx
	11	200	HTTP	ws-05dfb2c6186e4...	/crossdomainapprest/_layouts/15/AppWebProxy.aspx
	12	200	HTTP	ws-05dfb2c6186e4...	/CrossDomainAppREST/_api/web/lists

And you see in the Fiddler trace how the calls are being made to AppWebProxy.

END EXERCISE: Cross Domain REST Call

Well this was fun! We just wrote a simple app that used REST API to make cross domain calls. We saw that SharePoint has a standard mechanism of being able to do this via something called as the AppWebProxy. The code we wrote was standard REST code, except we piggybacked on SP.RequestExecutor.

The Chrome Control

You just saw an example of making cross domain calls using REST API. The code example was quite functional, but much like your first girlfriend it's quite ugly. Where did all that pretty SharePoint branding go? The answer is, all that branding won't come into your App, unless you use something called as the "Chrome control".

The fun thing is, cross domain calls are also possible in CSOM. In fact, CSOM understands such cross domain stuff. So let's go ahead and look at another example where I will use CSOM to load some data from the host web using CSOM. Additionally, this is also a great time for me to introduce the chrome control.

BEGIN EXERCISE: Cross Domain CSOM and Chrome Control

In this exercise, I will write a simple app that executes a cross domain CSOM call. In addition I will use the chrome control to view the app branded in the host web's SharePoint site's look and feel and color etc.

Start by creating a SharePoint hosted SharePoint 2013 app called ChromeControlCrossDomainCSOM.

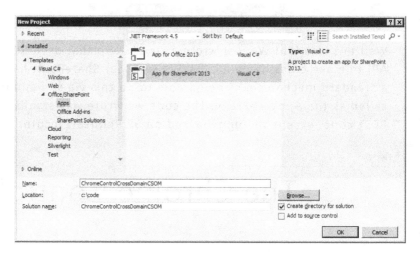

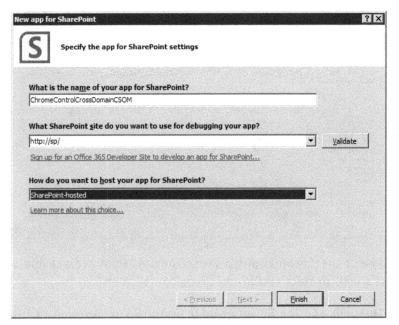

Once the app gets created, we need to do some cleanup. The cleanup is mostly because we wish to demonstrate that everything we do here can be done via just simple client side code.

Select and delete the following files,

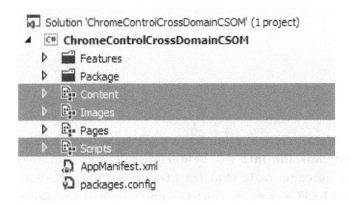

Next, in the solution add an empty asp.net 4 website as shown below,

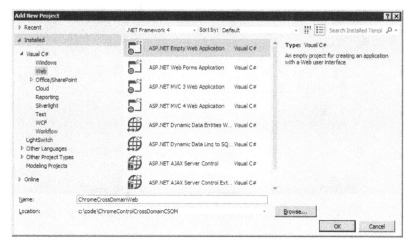

Select the ChromeControlCrossDomainCSOM project and set it's web project to ChromeCrossDomainWeb

This will add the Scripts folder and the TokenHelper.cs files in ChromeCrossDomainWeb, you can go ahead and delete them.

Finally, open the AppManifest.xml and change,

```
<AppPrincipal>
    <AutoDeployedWebApplication />
</AppPrincipal>
```

To ..

```
<AppPrincipal>
    <Internal AllowedRemoteHostUrl="~remoteAppUrl" />
</AppPrincipal>
```

NOTE: Effectively what you have done here is, you have changed your app into a provider hosted app, with no server side code. Note that the steps are a bit different from the REST example – but the end result is the same.

And change the start page to

```
<StartPage>~remoteAppUrl/ChromeCrossDomain.html?
{StandardTokens}&amp;SPHostTitle={HostTitle}</St
artPage>
```

Next, in the ChromeControlCrossDomainCSOM project add a new list as shown below,

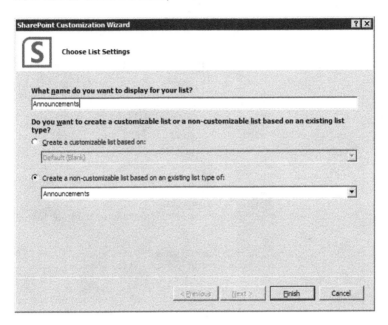

Open the Elements.xml for this list, and specify some data,

```xml
<?xml version="1.0" encoding="utf-8"?>
<Elements xmlns="http://schemas.microsoft.com/sharepoint/">
  <ListInstance Title="Announcements"
                OnQuickLaunch="TRUE"
                TemplateType="104"
                FeatureId="00bfea71-d1ce-42de-9c63-a44004ce0104"
                Url="Lists/Announcements"
                Description="My List Instance">
    <Data>
      <Rows>
        <Row>
          <Field Name="Title">Lorem ipsum 1</Field>
          <Field Name="Body">Sed ut perspiciatis, unde omnis iste natus e
        </Row>
        <Row>
          <Field Name="Title">Lorem ipsum 2</Field>
          <Field Name="Body">Sed ut perspiciatis, unde omnis iste natus e
        </Row>
        <Row>
          <Field Name="Title">Lorem ipsum 3</Field>
          <Field Name="Body">Sed ut perspiciatis, unde omnis iste natus e
        </Row>
        <Row>
          <Field Name="Title">Lorem ipsum 4</Field>
          <Field Name="Body">Sed ut perspiciatis, unde omnis iste natus e
        </Row>
        <Row>
          <Field Name="Title">Lorem ipsum 5</Field>
          <Field Name="Body">Sed ut perspiciatis, unde omnis iste natus e
        </Row>
      </Rows>
    </Data>
  </ListInstance>
</Elements>
```

Now what we intend to do here is, when the app launches, we intend to do a cross domain request using CSOM from the ChromeCrossDomainWeb project and read this announcements list. Additionally we will use the chrome control to brand our appweb.

Lets get rolling.

Open the ChromeCrossDomain.html file and add the following code in it,

```
<!DOCTYPE html>
<html xmlns="http://www.w3.org/1999/xhtml">
<head>
    <title>ClientOM Cross Domain</title>
    <script src="http://ajax.aspnetcdn.com/ajax/4.0/1/MicrosoftAjax.js" type="text/javascript"></script>
    <script type="text/javascript" src="http://ajax.aspnetcdn.com/ajax/jQuery/jquery-1.7.2.min.js"></script>
    <script type="text/javascript" src="ChromeLoader.js"></script>
    <script type="text/javascript" src="CrossDomainExec.js"></script>
</head>
<body>
    <div id="chrome_ctrl_placeholder"></div>
    <h1 class="ms-accentText">Main content</h1>
    <div id="renderAnnouncements"></div>
</body>
</html>
```

Note that I am using a SharePoint style called ms-accentText.

You will also note that I am referencing two JavaScript files in there, one is called ChromeLoader.js and the second is called CrossDomainExec.js. The ChromeLoader.js loads the Chrome control into the <div id="chrome_ctrl_placeholder"></div>. Lets examine that first.

In the ChromeLoader.js file, add the folliwng code,

```
var hostweburl;

//load the SharePoint resources
$(document).ready(function () {
    //Get the URI decoded URL.
    hostweburl =
        decodeURIComponent(
            getQueryStringParameter("SPHostUrl")
        );

    // The SharePoint js files URL are in the form:
    // app_web_url/_layouts/15/resource
    var scriptbase = hostweburl + "/_layouts/15/";

    // Load the js file and continue to the
    //    success handler
    $.getScript(scriptbase + "SP.UI.Controls.js", renderChrome)
});
```

You will see that we are loading the necessary scripts and calling method called renderChrome. The `getQueryStringParameter` method gets querystring parameter values as shown below

```
function getQueryStringParameter(paramToRetrieve) {
    var params =
        document.URL.split("?")[1].split("&");
    var strParams = "";
    for (var i = 0; i < params.length; i = i + 1) {
        var singleParam = params[i].split("=");
        if (singleParam[0] == paramToRetrieve)
            return singleParam[1];
    }
}
```

So the meat of the chrome control loading is in the renderChrome method, which is shown as below,

```
//Function to prepare the options and render the control
function renderChrome() {
    // The Help, Account and Contact pages receive the
    //   same query string parameters as the main page
    var options = {"appIconUrl": "siteIcon.png",
        "appTitle": "Chromecontrol-Crossdomain",
        "appHelpPageUrl": "Help.html?" + document.URL.split("?")[1],
        "settingsLinks": [
            {
                "linkUrl": "Account.html?" + document.URL.split("?")[1],
                "displayName": "Account settings"
            },
            {
                "linkUrl": "Contact.html?" + document.URL.split("?")[1],
                "displayName": "Contact us"
            }
        ]
    };

    var nav =
        new SP.UI.Controls.Navigation("chrome_ctrl_placeholder", options);
    nav.setVisible(true);
}
```

As you can see here, we are loading the chrome control in chrome_ctrl_placeholder, and we are specifying the Help, Account, and Contact pages in our rendering. When the chrome control loads, you will see these links rendered.

But before we run this, lets also go and finish out the logic for our app, which is to show announcements from the announcement list. That logic goes in CrossDomainExec.js and uses CSOM.

In this file, add the following code,

```
                                  ChromeLoader.js        ChromeCrossDomain.html      Elements.xml
    // The allAnnouncements variable is used by more than one
    //  function to retrieve and process the results.
    var allAnnouncements;
    var hostweburl;
    var appweburl;

    // Load the required SharePoint libraries
    $(document).ready(function () {
        //Get the URI decoded URLs.
        hostweburl =
            decodeURIComponent(
                getQueryStringParameter("SPHostUrl")
        );
        appweburl =
            decodeURIComponent(
                getQueryStringParameter("SPAppWebUrl")
        );

        // resources are in URLs in the form:
        // web_url/_layouts/15/resource
        var scriptbase = hostweburl + "/_layouts/15/";

        // Load the js files and continue to the successHandler
        $.getScript(scriptbase + "SP.Runtime.js",
            function () {
                $.getScript(scriptbase + "SP.js",
                    function () { $.getScript(scriptbase + "SP.RequestExecutor.js", execCrossDomainRequest); }
                );
            }
        );
    });
```

As you can tell, we are loading SP.RequestExecutor.js and when that loads, we call a method called execCrossDomainRequest. The execCrossDomainRequest method looks like as shown below,

```
   // Function to prepare and issue the request to get
   //  SharePoint data
function execCrossDomainRequest() {
    // context: The ClientContext object provides access to
    //        the web and lists objects.
    // factory: Initialize the factory object with the
    //        app web URL.
    var context = new SP.ClientContext(appweburl);
    var factory = new SP.ProxyWebRequestExecutorFactory(appweburl);
    context.set_webRequestExecutorFactory(factory);

    //Get the web and list objects
    //  and prepare the query
    var web = context.get_web();
    var list = web.get_lists().getByTitle("Announcements");
    var camlString =
        "<View><ViewFields>" +
            "<FieldRef Name='Title' />" +
            "<FieldRef Name='Body' />" +
        "</ViewFields></View>";

    var camlQuery = new SP.CamlQuery();
    camlQuery.set_viewXml(camlString);
    allAnnouncements = list.getItems(camlQuery);

    context.load(allAnnouncements, "Include(Title, Body)");

    // Execute the query with all the previous
    // options and parameters
    context.executeQueryAsync(successHandler, errorHandler);
}
```

Here we are executing a simple CAML Query, and if the method succeeds we call a success handler as shown below,

```
function successHandler(data, req) {
    var announcementsHTML = "";
    var enumerator = allAnnouncements.getEnumerator();

    while (enumerator.moveNext()) {
        var announcement = enumerator.get_current();

        // The chrome control also makes the SharePoint
        // website's stylesheet available to your page
        announcementsHTML = announcementsHTML +
            "<p><h2 class='ms-accentText'>" + announcement.get_item("Title") +
            "</h2>" + announcement.get_item("Body") +
            "</p><hr>";
    }

    document.getElementById("renderAnnouncements").innerHTML =
        announcementsHTML;
}
```

Note that again I am using SharePoint styles here to render the elements. Go ahead and hit F5 to run this app, and verify that the app produces the following output,

Also verify that the help link and the navigation link shows up.

POTHOLE ALERT: The Help link doesn't seem to have an icon. I have no idea why. It was there in Beta cycles. I'm guessing this is a bug.

END EXERCISE: Cross Domain CSOM and Chrome Control

App Replacement Tokens

You can also see this on my blog at
http://blah.winsmarts.com/2013-2-
SharePoint_2013_apps_replacement_tokens.aspx.

A long time ago, I had written about replaceable parameters that are available for use in Standard SharePoint solution packages oriented code. With the introduction of apps, we have a slew of new replaceable parameters at our disposal. These can be split into two parts,

1. Those that are URL tokens, i.e. to the left of the Query String, and
2. Those that can be part of the Query String.

Additionally, their usage is restricted to whether they are being run in Full Page, Custom Action or as a Client WebPart. So the tokens that can be added as a part of the URL are,

Token	Description	Full Page	Custom Action	Client WebPart
~appWebUrl	The URL of the app web of an app for SharePoint. This token should be used only outside an app web. Within the app web itself, use ~**site** for the URL of the app web.	Yes	Yes	Yes
~controlTemplates	The URL of the ControlTemplates virtual folder for the current website.	No	No	No

Token	Description	Full Page	Custom Action	Client WebPart
~hostUrl	The URL of the host web.	No	No	Yes
~hostLogoUrl	The URL of the logo of the host web.	No	No	No
~layouts	The URL of the Layouts virtual folder for the current website.	No	No	No
~remoteAppUrl	The URL of a remote web application in an app for SharePoint. This token can be used in the app manifest only for autohosted apps. For provider-hosted apps, you must specify the URL. It can be used outside the app manifest for both provider-hosted and autohosted apps.	Yes	Yes	Yes
~site	The URL of the current website.	No	No	Yes
~sitecollection	The URL of the parent site collection of the current website.	No	No	Yes

And the Tokens that can be part of the Query String are as below,

Token	Description	Full Page	Custom Action	Client WebPart
{AppContextToken}	The OAuth context token for the app.	No	No	No

{AppWebUrl}	This token should be used only outside an app web. Within the app web itself, use {Site} for the URL of the app web.	Yes	Yes	Yes
{ClientTag}	The client cache control number (client tag) for the current website.	Yes	Yes	Yes
{HostLogoUrl}	The logo for the host web of an app for SharePoint.	Yes	Yes	Yes
{HostTitle}	The title of the host web of an app for SharePoint.	Yes	Yes	Yes
{HostUrl}	The URL of the host web of an app for SharePoint.	Yes	Yes	Yes
{ItemId}	The ID of an item in a list or library (an integer).	No	Yes	No
{ItemUrl}	The URL of the item being acted upon.	No	Yes	No
{Language}	This token can be used in an app part, specifically the Src property, only if it appears in the path part of the value, not the query string part.	Yes	Yes	Yes.
{ListId}	The ID of the current list (a GUID).	No	Yes	No
{ProductNumber}	The full build version number of the	Yes	Yes	Yes

SharePoint farm.

{RecurrenceId}	This token is not supported for use in the context menus of list items.	No	Yes	No
{RemoteAppUrl}	The URL of a remote web application in an app for SharePoint.	Yes	Yes	Yes
{Site}	The URL of the current website.	No	Yes	Yes
{SiteCollection}	The URL of the parent site of the current website.	No	Yes	Yes
{SiteUrl}	The URL of the current website.	No	Yes	No
{Source}	The HTTP Request URL.	No	Yes	No
{StandardTokens}	This combines five other tokens. SPHostUrl, SPAppWebUrl, SPLanguage, SPClientTag and SPProductNumber. If there is no app web, the portion AppWebUrl is not present.			

On Premises S2S SharePoint App

Wow, you've gotten pretty good at writing apps. If you could describe your functionality using client side code, and assuming you know enough about REST API and CSOM, you're already an expert at writing such apps. But what if you wanted to involve server side code?

Well, that is where the S2S and OAuth based apps come in.

Apps that involve server side code are a whole science in themselves. There is plenty to learn there. So, we will learn this in a crawl/walk/run fashion.

a) First, I will demonstrate how you can write an S2S app purely via Visual Studio, here Visual Studio will help us quite a bit. So we get to omit some steps

b) Then, I will demonstrate how you can package such an app and deploy it to production. By putting #a and #b together you will have the complete picture of how to author S2s on premises apps.

c) Finally, I will talk about Azure ACS based OAuth apps, where I will also have the opportunity to describe the security aspects of such apps.

So lets get rolling with understanding S2S basics.

The first high-trust app uses server to server protocol. Server to Server protocol is also used by Lync/Exchange etc. Apps piggy back upon that mechanism. High trust is not Full trust. Full trust means, do whatever you wish. High trust means, the App server is pre-trusted by SharePoint. This app server then authenticates the user, and simply tells SharePoint, hey the user is Daniel Craig.

And SharePoint blindly trusts this server and assumes the request is coming from Daniel Craig. The app still is running under the granted permissions, but the user identity is set to be Daniel craig, or whatever the App Server says.

At the time of writing this book, S2S is the only choice on-premises since automatically trusting the app via Azure ACS is not a choice on-premises. This also means that the context token provided by Azure ACS (I will talk about Azure ACS secured apps and context tokens later in this book), is not available in on-premises apps. As a result, you need to do some manual steps to trust the app using the server to server protocol.

You might wonder if app-store based provider hosted apps will be available since there are manual steps involved. Farm administrators are able to configure their farms in such a way that it can support a broader of apps, and the storefront will appropriately enable/disable apps that can be used on the configured on-premises environment.

It is worth noting however that the app itself, whether it is written or Office 365 or on Premises, is quite similar. The process of executing queries, the process of requesting app permissions is identical. It's just how you install the app that differs and how you gain security rights that differs. So for simple apps you can separate your logic into reusable libraries and theoretically create an app that can work in both OAuth and S2S.

Let's get our feet wet with writing a simple On-Premises provider hosted app.

Begin Exercise: Writing an On-Premises Provider Hosted App

In this exercise, we will write a simple app that executes a cross domain CSOM call. However, in this example we will have the option of having some code in a separate web application. This separate web application will be responsible for serving the application and it will be registered in SharePoint as an app.

The interesting thing here is that both the client-side, and the server side will be able to make calls into the server. We already know how the client side can make cross-domain calls. Let's examine in this exercise how server side code can make calls into the SharePoint server. Additionally, how does security work in this setting?

For security, we need to first need to generate a certificate. Start InetMgr, and select the machine name, and select server certificates,

When in this applet, choose to create a self-signed certificate as shown below,

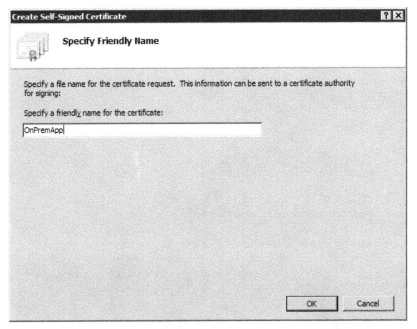

www.winsmarts.com | 113 | P a g e

Next, export this certificate to a directory, I exported mine to c:\code. First export it as a .cer without the private key, second as a .pfx with the private key – remember the password here, my password was p@ssword1.

Next, using these certs, lets go ahead and get an issuer ID using the following PowerShell script,

```
Add-PSSnapin "Microsoft.SharePoint.PowerShell"

$issuerID = [System.Guid]::NewGuid().ToString()

Write-Host "Issuer ID is :" $issuerID

$targetSiteUrl = "http://sp"

$targetSite = Get-SPSite $targetSiteUrl

$realm = Get-SPAuthenticationRealm -
ServiceContext $targetSite

$registeredIssuerName = $issuerID + '@' +
$realm

$publicCertificatePath =
"c:\code\onpremapp.cer"

$publicCertificate = Get-PfxCertificate
$publicCertificatePath

$secureTokenIssuer = New-
SPTrustedSecurityTokenIssuer -Name $issuerID -
RegisteredIssuerName $registeredIssuerName -
Certificate $publicCertificate -IsTrustBroker


$serviceConfig = Get-
SPSecurityTokenServiceConfig

$serviceConfig.AllowOAuthOverHttp = $true

$serviceConfig.Update()
```

This script will print out a GUID, this is the issuer ID – note it down, you'll need it when you create the Visual Studio project.

There is also something else you need to create called as the App Principal – Visual Studio will create this on the fly for you – so you don't need to run the below script on your development machine, but when you wish to deploy this app, you will need to run the following powershell script to create an app principal.

```
$appDisplayName = "OnPremApp"
$clientID = [System.Guid]::NewGuid().ToString()
$fullAppPrincipalIdentifier = $clientID + '@' +
$realm
$registeredAppPrincipal = Register-
SPAppPrincipal -NameIdentifier
$fullAppPrincipalIdentifier -Site
$targetSite.RootWeb -DisplayName
$AppDisplayName
Write-Host "Client ID is :" $clientID
```

Once the App principal is created, the above script will give you a client ID – you will need to put this in specific places in appmanifest.xml and the web.config of the on-prem app. This is a deployment only step – not needed in development environment. Visual studio generates the app principal on the fly for you.

I will show the usage of this in the next exercise.

With the issuer id ready, (mine was 63d8f881-3fe8-46bb-ada3-83724cb4e4dc), start Visual Studio 2012 and create a new SharePoint 2013 app, call it "OnPremApp" but this time, and choose it to be a Provider Hosted app as shown below,

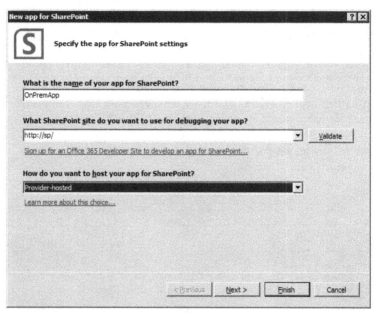

In the next screen, choose the .pfx certificate you had exported earlier and in the issuerID the issuer ID you have already created, this can be seen as below

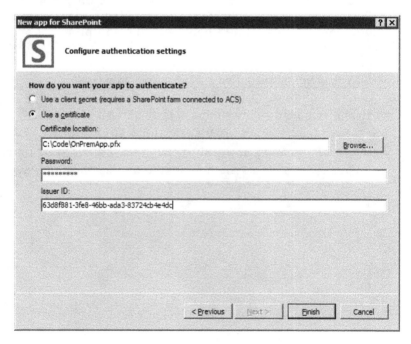

Your project will get created as shown below,

Note that here you have two projects, one that is the app – second that is the provider hosted portion of the app.

Now what we intend to do here in this app, is demonstrate both client side code and server side code, making secure cross domain requests to the hostweb.

Lets get rolling.

First, double click the AppManifest.xml and change the QueryString as follows,

Icon:	OnPremApp/AppIcon.png

Start page:	OnPremAppWeb/Pages/Default.aspx

Query string:	{StandardTokens}?SPHostTitle={HostTitle}

Next, go to the permissions tab, and change the permissions as shown below,

Next, go to the code behind of Default.aspx in your provider app, and change the code to as shown below,

```
protected void Page_Load(object sender, EventArgs e)
{
    // The following code gets the client context and Title property by using TokenHelper.
    // To access other properties, you may need to request permissions on the host web.

    Uri hostWeb = new Uri(Request.QueryString["SPHostUrl"]);

    using (var clientContext = TokenHelper.GetS2SClientContextWithWindowsIdentity(hostWeb, Request.LogonUserIdentity))
    {
        var web = clientContext.Web;
        clientContext.Load(web.ContentTypes);
        clientContext.ExecuteQuery();
        ContentTypesList.DataSource = web.ContentTypes;
        ContentTypesList.DataBind();
    }
}
```

The "ContentTypesList" is a control you need to add in the Default.aspx, edit the "body" tag of Default.aspx as shown below,

```
<body>
    <div id="SPChrome"></div>
    <form id="form1" runat="server">
        <div style="margin: 20px;">
            <asp:Repeater ID="ContentTypesList" runat="server">
                <ItemTemplate>
                    <div class="contentRow"><%# Eval("Name") %> : <%# Eval("Id") %></div>
                </ItemTemplate>
            </asp:Repeater>
        </div>
    </form>
</body>
```

That SPChrome div, lets go ahead and set it up with the
Chrome control, add the following JavaScript in the page to
accomplish that,

```
<head id="Head1" runat="server">
    <title></title>
    <script src="../Scripts/jquery-1.7.1.min.js"></script>
    <script type="text/javascript">
        var hostWebUrl;
        var hostLayoutsUrl;
        $(document).ready(function () {
            hostWebUrl = decodeURIComponent(getParameterByName("SPHostUrl"));
            hostLayoutsUrl = hostWebUrl + "/_layouts/15/";
            $.getScript(hostLayoutsUrl + "SP.UI.Controls.js", function () {
                var nav = new SP.UI.Controls.Navigation("SPChrome", { "appTitle": "On Premises Provider Hosted App" });
                nav.setVisible(true);
            });
        });

        function getParameterByName(name) {
            var match = RegExp('[?&]' + name + '=([^&]*)')
                .exec(window.location.search);
            return match && decodeURIComponent(match[1].replace(/\+/g, ' '));
        }
    </script>
</head>
```

Now, open the web.config of the OnPremAppWeb project,
note that the "ClientId" value is blank. Now, hit F5 to
deploy and run your app. You may be greeted with a dialog
as shown below,

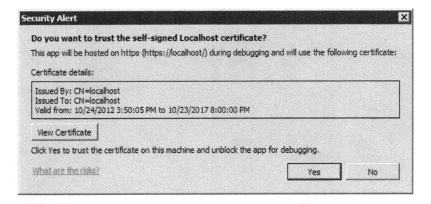

Just hit "Yes" to trust this certificate.

You would note that soon as the app is installed, Visual Studio detects that the ClientID has changed and prompts you to reload the web.config in Visual Studio

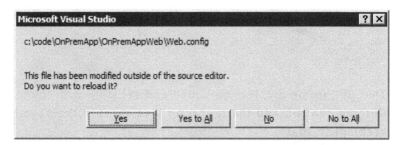

Verify that the ClientID now has a value in it.

In the browser, go ahead and trust your app

Do you trust OnPremApp?

Let it read items in this site.

Let it access basic information about the users of this site.

OnPremApp

Verify that you are able to run the app as shown below,

On Premises Provider Hosted App

System : 0x
Common Indicator Columns : 0x00A7470EADF4194E2E9ED1031B61DA0884
Fixed Value based Status Indicator : 0x00A7470EADF4194E2E9ED1031B61DA088401
SharePoint List based Status Indicator : 0x00A7470EADF4194E2E9ED1031B61DA088402
Excel based Status Indicator : 0x00A7470EADF4194E2E9ED1031B61DA088403
SQL Server Analysis Services based Status Indicator : 0x00A7470EADF4194E2E9ED1031B61DA088404
Item : 0x01
Circulation : 0x01000F389E14C9CE4CE486270B9D4713A5D6
New Word : 0x010018F21907ED4E401CB4F14422ABC65304
Category : 0x010019ACC57FBA4146AFA4C822E719824BED
Site Membership : 0x010027FC2137D8DE4B00A40E14346D070D52
Community Member : 0x010027FC2137D8DE4B00A40E14346D070D5201
WorkflowServiceDefinition : 0x01002A2479FF33DD4BC3B1533A012B653717
Health Analyzer Rule Definition : 0x01003A8AA7A4F53046158C5ABD98036A01D5
Resource : 0x01004C9F4486FBF54864A7B0A33D02AD19B1
Official Notice : 0x01007CE30DD1206047728BAFD1C39A850120
Phone Call Memo : 0x0100807FBAC5EB8A4653B8D24775195B5463

Awesome! You now have server side code reading stuff from the SharePoint site. The possibilities are endless.

End Exercise: Writing an On-Premises Provider Hosted App

Fabulous! We just wrote our app. What was interesting here is that Visual Studio helped me all along the way here. It created a ClientID (sometimes known as the AppID) for me. The idea here is that with one issuer id, you can have many client ids.

Deploying your S2S app

You just wrote an S2S app in Visual Studio. Impressive, but not enough! The issue is, Visual studio helped you out, it generated the client ID for you and it registered an App Principal for you. What do you need to do to deploy this app in production? On a well-known URL, pre-trusted, and ready to go! Lets find out.

BEGIN EXERCISE: Deploying an S2S App

To proceed with this exercise, you should have already successfully have completed the previous exercise where I demonstrated how you can write a S2S app using Visual Studio.

Now that you have written such an app, we need to host it on your network. How do we do it?

There are two steps,

a) Generate a client id and register an App principal.
b) Host the app with this new client id, and update your app to reflect the client ID.

Go ahead and run the following script to generate a client ID

```
Add-PSSnapin
"Microsoft.SharePoint.PowerShell"
$targetSiteUrl = "http://sp"
$targetSite = Get-SPSite $targetSiteUrl
$realm = Get-SPAuthenticationRealm -
ServiceContext $targetSite


$appDisplayName = "OnPremApp"
$clientID =
[System.Guid]::NewGuid().ToString()
$fullAppPrincipalIdentifier = $clientID +
'@' + $realm
$registeredAppPrincipal = Register-
SPAppPrincipal -NameIdentifier
$fullAppPrincipalIdentifier -Site
```

```
$targetSite.RootWeb -DisplayName
$AppDisplayName

Write-Host "Client ID is :" $clientID
```

Once you have generated the client id, go ahead and update it in both the web.config of the provider hosted app and the appmanifest.xml as shown below,

```xml
<AppPrincipal>
    <RemoteWebApplication ClientId="ed76be61-a7bd-4a2b-af40-509844dc4e9f" />
</AppPrincipal>
```

```xml
</system.web>
<appSettings>
    <add key="ClientId" value="ed76be61-a7bd-4a2b-af40-509844dc4e9f" />
    <add key="ClientSecret" value="gDcjXEw/uvomGyI0X/uJIcPnOrdJ+tmapcn4KmE9YZg=" />
    <add key="ClientSigningCertificatePath" value="C:\Code\onpremapp.pfx" />
    <add key="ClientSigningCertificatePassword" value="p@ssword1" />
    <add key="IssuerId" value="2cbb5b93-2657-4f67-98d9-2ea77c80170c" />
```

Now, we need to host the provider hosted web app. Go to inetmgr, and create a new website on port 81 as shown below,

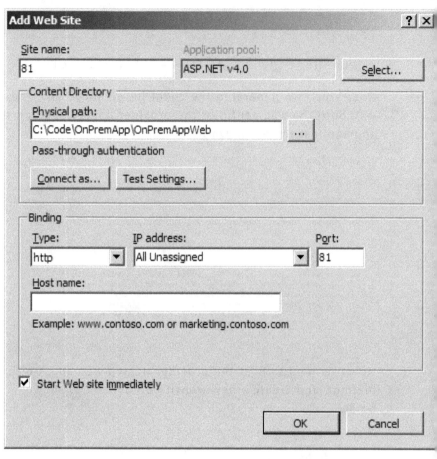

Change the authentication settings of this app as follows,

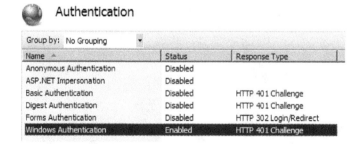

So your app is now running on http://sp:81. Visit the
appmanifest.xml and modify the start URL of the app as
shown below,

```
    >
 ⊟  <Properties>
      <Title>OnPremApp</Title>
      <StartPage>http://sp:81/Pages/Default.aspx?{StandardTokens}?SPHostTitle={HostTitle}</StartPage>
    </Properties>
```

Next, go ahead and right click and publish the app. In the first screen, go ahead and enter a name for your publish profile,

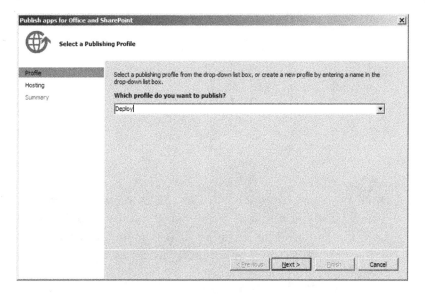

Now we intend to host the app internally in the enterprise app catalog, so go ahead and fill the next dialog as shown below,

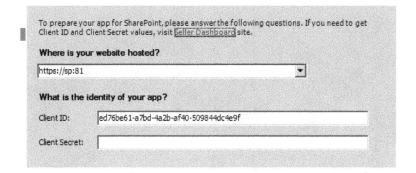

Now you may ask that your site was hosted on http://sp:81, but you are typing https://sp:81. This dialog requires you to

type in https – but it won't modify your appmanifest.xml. You could use https, and that is what you should do in production, but for development http is just fine.

Once the app is published, go ahead and upload it to your app catalog as shown below,

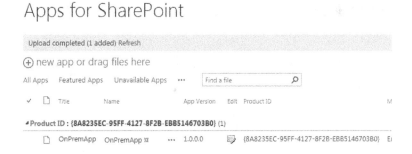

Once the app is uploaded to the app catalog, go to your http://sp SharePoint site, and ensure that you don't already have the OnPremApp installed. If it is installed, go ahead and uninstall it. Then, go ahead and add an app as shown below,

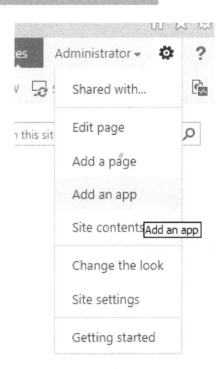

Look for the OnPremApp and add it to your site as shown below,

Apps you can add   Newest   Name

OnPremApp   Document Library   Form Library
App Details   App Details   App Details

Once you try to add the app, you will also have to trust it as usual,

Then the app will go through the usual installation process,

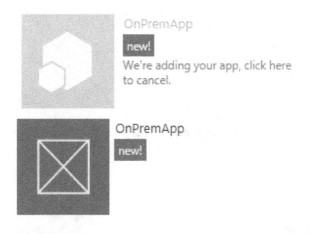

And once the app is installed, you should be able to see it running as shown below,

On Premises Provider Hosted App

System : 0x
Common Indicator Columns : 0x00A7470EADF4194E2E9ED1031B61DA0884
Fixed Value based Status Indicator : 0x00A7470EADF4194E2E9ED1031B61DA088401
SharePoint List based Status Indicator : 0x00A7470EADF4194E2E9ED1031B61DA088402
Excel based Status Indicator : 0x00A7470EADF4194E2E9ED1031B61DA088403
SQL Server Analysis Services based Status Indicator : 0x00A7470EADF4194E2E9ED1031B61DA08840
Item : 0x01
Circulation : 0x01000F389E14C9CE4CE486270B9D4713A5D6
New Word : 0x010018F21907ED4E401CB4F14422ABC65304
Category : 0x010019ACC57FBA4146AFA4C822E719824BED
Site Membership : 0x010027FC2137D8DE4B00A40E14346D070D52
Community Member : 0x010027FC2137D8DE4B00A40E14346D070D5201
WorkflowServiceDefinition : 0x01002A2479FF33DD4BC3B1533A012B653717
Health Analyzer Rule Definition : 0x01003A8AA7A4F53046158C5ABD98036A01D5
Resource : 0x01004C9F4486FBF54864A7B0A33D02AD19B1
Official Notice : 0x01007CE30DD1206047728BAFD1C39A850120
Phone Call Memo : 0x0100807FBAC5EB8A4653B8D24775195B5463

END EXERCISE: Deploying an S2S App

Great! You know quite a bit about Apps now. But before I go much further, I must tell you something very very important. Did you note that the deploy wizard in Visual Studio wouldn't let you type anything except https? I haven't had much of an opportunity to talk about app security, but for now let me just say, Apps and in fact SharePoint 2013, without https is an unacceptable level of security even on an intranet. In other words, **a production SharePoint 2013 installation must use https**.

Wow that was fun! We had an ASP.NET app working as an app, requesting permissions and reading a list of content types from SharePoint. We even deployed it nicely on IIS and installed it properly into the enterprise app catalog. That is all great, but, what about Office 365 and OAuth?

Before we go there, lets chat a bit about App Security

App Security

If you haven't already, please read the section about App Permissions before reading this.

Security in SharePoint can be thought of as two big buckets —

a) User Security which is largely unchanged from SharePoint 2010 except that Claims based auth is now default and the FedAuth cookie never leaves the server now.
b) App Security which is brand new.

There are three kinds of App Security,

a) Internal authentication: where you piggy back on the user's identity to do your stuff. The request would check for a SAML token to know the user's identity, if the user has permissions to do something the request goes through, otherwise it doesn't. You would use internal authentication in three scenarios, client-side calls from pages in the app web, Client-side calls from pages in remote web which use cross domain library or when the HostWeb Server-side code calls to app web
b) External Authentication using OAuth
c) External Authentication using S2S.

The main difference between internal authentication and external authentication is that in external authentication, you are required to manage an access token. An access token is what establishes your app's secure identity. There is an authentication dance you need to go through in OAuth before you get the access token.

In internal authentication, SAML token is enough – there is no need for an access token.

Additionally, when you install the App, the app gets an identity. This is called as the **App Principal**. This is very much like the user principal, except you don't see it in the UI. Every securable object that the app has rights to has the app principal on it. Deleting the securable object removes the right, restoring the object restores the right. What if the app was uninstalled between a delete and a restore? Usually this would be a problem but the access token that contains the apps identity (usually in addition to the user's identity) is good for only an hour, so it's not such a big deal.

There are many pages built into SharePoint that help you manage App security. These pages are not visible in the UI, but they are there. Type in the URL, you'll find them.

_layouts/15/AppRegNew.aspx, is used to create or register an App ID, the same thing you did in PowerShell, except through a web page.

	Create	Cancel

App Information

The app's information, including app id, secret, title, hosting uri and redirect uri.

App Id:

[   ] Generate

App Secret:

[   ] Generate

Title:

[   ]

App Domain:

[   ]

Example: "www.contoso.com"

Redirect URI:

[   ]

Example: "https://www.contoso.com/default.aspx"

	Create	Cancel

Note that there is also a place to write in a Redirect URI. This is used for on the fly permissions, which currently the TokenHelper.cs has support for only ACS connected installations. This is an interesting limitation currently since the redirect URI must be registerd with ACS, but ACS cannot register http://localhost , in other words, you develop against an internet facing URI, that's not so nice! And what about a QA->Prod story, again not so nice. I'm sure better patterns/workarounds will emerge for this, but this is what we have right now.

_layouts/15/AppInv.aspx, is used to grant to an app or view permissions of an already installed app as long as you know it's app id,

Create	Cancel

App Id and Title
The app's identity and its title.

App Id:
[   ] [Lookup]

Title:
[   ]

App Domain:
[   ]
Example: "www.contoso.com"

Redirect URL:
[   ]
Example: "https://www.contoso.com/default.aspx"

App's Permission Request XML
The permission requred by the app.

Permission Request XML:
[   ]

Create	Cancel

_layouts/15/AppPrincipals.aspx, shows you the currently registered app principals.

Test   ✏ EDIT LINKS

Site Settings ▸ Site Collection App Permissions ⓘ

App Display Name↑	App Identifier
✕ SharePoint	i:0i.t|ms.sp.ext|00000003-0000-0ff1-ce00-000000000000@74bdf936-923b-49bf-a8d3-459f5b4349ef

POTHOLE ALERT: I found a little issue with the AppPrincipals page. It only shows me App Principals that are currently in use. In other words if I was futzing around my dev environment, and created a bunch of App Principals that I am not using currently, well they just don't show up here. I can only view them via the SP Object model or PowerShell. Well that sucks. Be careful of creating such App Principals on production.

And finally, **_layouts/15/AppRedirect.aspx** is called during the installation of an app.

App Authentication in the cloud

In the previous example you saw an example of installing and writing an App that uses server side code outside of SharePoint – commonly known as "Provider hosted apps". When you work with Office 365, you can really enhance the functionality of Office 365 by writing such apps. But compared to on-premises non-SharePoint hosted apps, Office 365 non-SharePoint hosted apps have three important differences you need to know about,

    a) You have the option of writing Provider Hosted apps, or Azure hosted apps. Both have a server side component outside of SharePoint but the Azure hosted apps are lesser headache, because the server side is provisioned for you automatically in Azure when the app is installed. Note that this Azure hosting is a bit of a black-box to us. It is something that the Office 365 team worked out with Azure, it's not something that we get to play with directly, like Azure cloud services.

b) Office 365 use an OAuth based Authentication dance that involves Azure ACS to grant or deny access to the functionality being requested.

c) And Office 365 doesn't offer as many permissions as on-premises apps.

Let's begin by understanding this authentication dance.

Azure ACS and SharePoint authentication dance

The Azure ACS and Office 365 authentication dance is described as below,

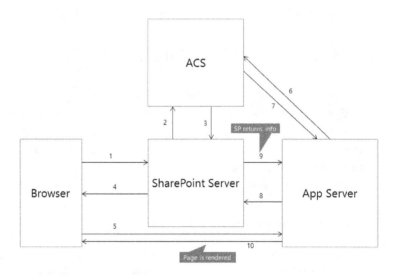

1. User accesses the SharePoint server
2. SharePoint detects an app on the page. SharePoint asks ACS to create & sign a context token. Context token is context info + authorization code.

3. ACS mints a signed context token. It contains an App Secret that the App knows and ACS knows. You receive this secret when your app is registered in the seller dashboard

4. SharePoint renders the page with an IFRAME passing the **context token** to the IFRAME. The context token also contains a **refresh token**.

5. The IFRAME loads a page from the App Server. The IFRAME passes the **context token** to the app server.

6. App Server validates the **context token** using the secret. It can also use the **refresh token** to request an access token to access SP artifacts.

7. ACS returns the **access token**

8. App Server can make a call to the SP server with the access token written in the HTTP authorization header.

As you can see, there are three tokens involved here,

- **Context Token**: Expires every 12 hours, can store in a cookie, but you will need to use appredirect.aspx to get refresh an expired token. Cached either as a cookie or AppFabric cache. The CacheKey is calculated as, UserNameId + "," + UserNameIdIssuer + "," + ApplicationId + "," + Realm

- **Refresh Token**: Good for a year. Apps can store refresh tokens.

- **Access Token**: Good for an hour

Therefore, when you write your apps, and you wish to use the client object model or REST API in making a cross-domain call into SharePoint, you will need the context token. You can request the token as follows,

```
SharePointContextTokencontextToken=TokenHelp
er.ReadAndValidateContextToken(contextTokenS
tring,Request.Url.Authority);
```

The context token looks like as shown below,

{"typ":"JWT","alg":"none"}.{"aud":"ee3c6eeb-666b-4c5e-b5ec-2665b260709e/sphvm-5265:41688@eff13d
0d-67b5-411b-8e8a-9e0189fa7558","iss":"00000001-0000-0000-c000-000000000000@eff13d0d-67b5-411b-
8e8a-9e0189fa7558","nbf":"1334091996","exp":"1334135196","nameid":"s-1-5-21-2127521184-16040129
20-1887927527-415149","actor":"00000003-0000-0ff1-ce00-000000000000@eff13d0d-67b5-411b-8e8a-9e0
189fa7558","identityprovider":"urn:office:idp:activedirectory",
"appctx":"{\"CacheKey\":\"r2qTqJITfRWLO26QvJOQsjH61CiLTSSqLZY70kpr4vk=\",\"SecurityTokenService
Uri\":
\"https://accounts-int-sn1-004.accesscontrol.aadint.windows-int.net/tokens/OAuth/2\"}","refresh
token":"IAAAAGAIMAusi3wdFTCCf8pHrgfEWjNImZjvkUEzxV4jeN+SoH8GIHL40kvCMA1moSd0VFkFd9fJymgx/MY
qt5YJn2aI1cYFYWLXPCk6vUfffJ/yIam6L53JY97Quo1ajPgFOPYb9TIIp+rONjPoOst6YuC/azQ/Bz+NbnRpv/zslHDhuR
IEsdyj4VZRGrDKj+Tj9A1QhEjWiV5a
AcJSQ/kUS2JXWcvJuXUIB60h4hFnt+FVxXx28MgOWJt7JDchZSPaHpcjjeepLUM41XspbAbyJ8nt768/ItmkfrwuLLc3U1H
mCdUYJUmyWQr4jy04ob+ukWq7SfUsoi
bsH6SUtGB8aCB0xdyp0OnY8XNEbPTyVRkSR2Cln8OjvuwH+bNBtL5skIvbBFEF1fpkAxroRZxwPcTTa4GImH89Q+

You can see the shaded portion is the cache key.

The context token can contain the following information,

Notation	Description	Fields	Example value
aud	aud is short for "audience", meaning the principal for which the token is intended. The format is {target client Id}/{target URL authority}@{ta rget realm}.	**Target client Id**	a044e184-7de2-4d05-aacf-52118008c44e
		App domain	contoso:122
realm	Tenancy	**realm**	040f2415-e6e3-4480-96ce-26ef73275f73
iss	iss is short for "issuer". It represents the principal that created the	**ACS**	00000001-0000-0000-c000-000000000000

	token. The GUID **0000000 1-0000-0000- c000- 00000000000 0** is ACS. The format is {ACS}@{ target realm}.		
nbf	nbf is short for "not before". It represents the time at which the token*starts* being valid.	**nbf**	1335822895
exp	exp is short for "expiration". It represents the time after which the token is no longer valid.	**exp**	1335866095
nameid	nameid is a unique identifier for the user the token is issued on behalf of. The format of the value indicates where the user	**nameid**	s-1-5-21-2127521184-...

	identity is coming from (that is, which claims identity provider the user identity is coming from).		
CacheKey	See the FAQ about cache key in this section.		KQAlUpDUD0sm5Tr83U...
Actor	Actor is the application principal identity for SharePoint 2013 Preview, Exchange Server 2013 Preview, or Microsoft Lync 2013.	SharePoint 2013 Preview	00000003-0000-0ff1-ce00-000000000000
refreshtoken	The refresh token for the app.	**refreshtoken**	IAAAAC1Lv5w0OrcFAmJx0xk6...

There is also the facility built in to get a short client context. Sometimes external WCF services are reused between SharePoint and non-SharePoint apps. They don't need a full context token. They can simply use the TokenHelper.ReadAndValidateContextToken() to differentiate between SharePoint callers or non-SharePoint callers. If the context starts with **00000003-0000-0ff1-ce00-**

000000000000, then the originator is either SharePoint, Exchange or Lync.

S2S and SharePoint authentication dance

I wonder if you can even call it a dance, this is really much simpler as shown in the diagram below,

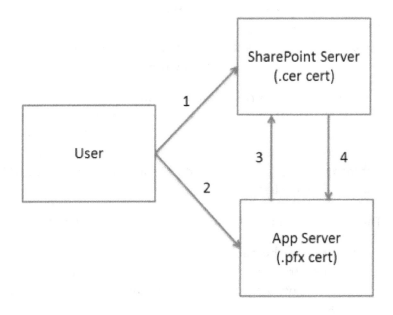

1. The user requests a SharePoint page which then loads the app –
2. SharePoint authenticates the user, the app also authenticates the user.
3. From here, the app server simply forwards the identity of the user to the SharePoint server, and
4. The SharePoint server trusts the identity with the help of the certificates, and offers the content.

See, much simpler! Except you have to setup the S2S server first.

Provider-Hosted Apps in Office 365 using Azure ACS

I hope you made it this far because I have a good news for you. You know that complex authentication dance between Office 365 and Azure ACS, well you never have to worry about it. Writing an auto hosted app is SO MUCH simpler than actually understanding how it works.

Okay, I'll go on the record and say this – I think the biggest reason Microsoft invested in apps, was the cloud version of SharePoint that comes with Office365. And who could blame them? It makes total sense both for customers and Microsoft. The provider hosted apps also work in Office 365 – only, they are better! :)

There are two kinds of provider hosted apps in Office 365.

1. Provider hosted, where you provide the hosting infrastructure, these apps are quite similar to what you have already seen except authentication of the apps.
2. Azure hosted, where you specify all of the back-end website details in the app package itself, and when the App is installed, SharePoint will provision the website in Azure for you. Note that this is a blackbox, it is not the Azure we usually use – it is something that Office365 and Azure have negotiated on getting things to work more seamlessly for us.

The biggest difference between Office365 apps and On-Prem apps, is authentication, so lets look at how apps are authenticated in Azure using Azure ACS.

With a solid understanding how security works in SharePoint, now let's switch our focus on writing apps for Office 365.

Provider hosted apps for Office 365 are quite similar to writing them for on-premises. Barring a few details around security and how you request the client token, or some permission details, the process of writing them, and the tooling is quite similar. And most of those complexities are abstracted for you in TokenHelper.cs anyway.

Therefore, it is reasonable to say that apps that you wrote for on-premises, in many cases (not all) will easily migrate to Office 365.

Therefore in this section, I am going to show how you can write a provider hosted app, and then migrate it to Office 365. In migration to Office 365, I will first show a provider hosted app, followed by an autohosted/azure hosted app . I will finally demonstrate how you can develop Office 365 apps, without even requiring a SharePoint developer machine.

What? No SharePoint developer machine required to write Office 365 apps? You must be kidding! No I am not. I'll prove it, in the next exercise.

You may be wondering, who pays for the automatically provisioned Azure website? Well, it is yet to be decided at the time of writing this book. In fact, this technology of autohosted apps, as cool as it is, will remain in preview after SharePoint RTMs. Microsoft will eventually release pricing details and other such relevant details. Still, it is compelling enough that we must learn it, it promises to be a valuable asset especially if you're targeting Office 365.

Begin Exercise: Writing autohosted apps for Office 365

In this exercise, I will write a simple app that executes a cross domain CSOM call. However, in this example I will have the option of having some code in a separate web application. This separate web application will be responsible for serving the application and it will be registered in SharePoint as an app.

What is different between this example and the previous is that the separate web application in this example sits in Azure. Not only does it sit in azure, it gets auto provisioned for you when you install the app and removed when you uninstall the app. Fancy!

Start by launching Visual Studio 2012 and creating an App for SharePoint 2013 as shown below,

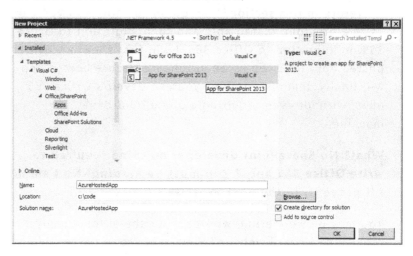

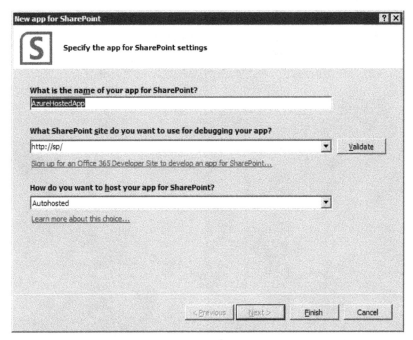

The way we develop Autohosted applications is that we develop and debug the app locally – but – the app itself targets Office 365. So here is what you need to do,

a) Sign up for an Office 365 site, and then,
b) In the properties of your app, change the URL to your SharePoint Office 365 developer site

Next, grant Web \ Read access to your App

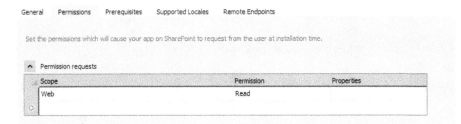

We are now ready to write our app logic. The logic of the app is very simple – the app web (running in azure, but for now running locally), will show a button – when you click on the button, it will show various details of the host web like the current username, user list etc. So, lets craft up the UI first, the contents of the form in Default.aspx of the Web App (AzureHostedAppWeb) is shown as below,

```
<div>
    <asp:ScriptManager ID="ScriptManager1" runat="server" EnablePartialRendering="true" />
    <asp:UpdatePanel ID="PopulateData" runat="server" UpdateMode="Conditional">
        <ContentTemplate>
            <table border="1" cellpadding="10">
                <tr>
                    <th>
                        <asp:LinkButton ID="CSOM" runat="server" Text="Populate Data" OnClick="CSOM_Click" /></th>
                </tr>
                <tr>
                    <td>
                        <h2>SharePoint Site</h2>
                        <asp:Label runat="server" ID="WebTitleLabel" />
                        <h2>Current User:</h2>
                        <asp:Label runat="server" ID="CurrentUserLabel" />
                        <h2>Site Users</h2>
                        <asp:ListView ID="UserList" runat="server">
                            <ItemTemplate>
                                <asp:Label ID="UserItem" runat="server" Text="<%# Container.DataItem.ToString() %>"></asp:Label><br />
                            </ItemTemplate>
                        </asp:ListView>
                        <h2>Site Lists</h2>
                        <asp:ListView ID="ListList" runat="server">
                            <ItemTemplate>
                                <asp:Label ID="ListItem" runat="server" Text="<%# Container.DataItem.ToString() %>"></asp:Label><br />
                            </ItemTemplate>
                        </asp:ListView>
                    </td>
                </tr>
            </table>
        </ContentTemplate>
    </asp:UpdatePanel>
</div>
```

Next, go to the code behind and in the Page_Load add the following code,

```
protected void Page_Load(object sender, EventArgs e)
{
    TokenHelper.TrustAllCertificates();
    string contextTokenString = TokenHelper.GetContextTokenFromRequest(Request);

    if (contextTokenString != null)
    {
        contextToken =
            TokenHelper.ReadAndValidateContextToken(contextTokenString, Request.Url.Authority);

        sharepointUrl = new Uri(Request.QueryString["SPHostUrl"]);
        accessToken =
            TokenHelper.GetAccessToken(contextToken, sharepointUrl.Authority).AccessToken;
        CSOM.CommandArgument = accessToken;

    }
    else if (!IsPostBack)
    {
        Response.Write("Could not find a context token.");
        return;
    }
}
```

With the accessToken available, next lets write the code for CSOM_Click,

```
protected void CSOM_Click(object sender, EventArgs e)
{
    string commandAccessToken = ((LinkButton)sender).CommandArgument;
    RetrieveWithCSOM(commandAccessToken);
    WebTitleLabel.Text = siteName;
    CurrentUserLabel.Text = currentUser;
    UserList.DataSource = listOfUsers;
    UserList.DataBind();
    ListList.DataSource = listOfLists;
    ListList.DataBind();

}
```

Finally, here is the code for the RetreiveWithCSOM,

```
// This method retrieves information about the host web by using the CSOM.
private void RetrieveWithCSOM(string accessToken)
{
    if (IsPostBack) sharepointUrl = new Uri(Request.QueryString["SPHostUrl"]);

    ClientContext clientContext =
            TokenHelper.GetClientContextWithAccessToken(
                sharepointUrl.ToString(), accessToken);

    //Load the properties for the web object.
    Web web = clientContext.Web;
    clientContext.Load(web);
    clientContext.ExecuteQuery();

    //Get the site name.
    siteName = web.Title;

    //Get the current user.
    clientContext.Load(web.CurrentUser);
    clientContext.ExecuteQuery();
    currentUser = clientContext.Web.CurrentUser.LoginName;

    //Load the lists from the Web object.
    ListCollection lists = web.Lists;
    clientContext.Load<ListCollection>(lists);
    clientContext.ExecuteQuery();

    //Load the current users from the Web object.
    UserCollection users = web.SiteUsers;
    clientContext.Load<UserCollection>(users);
    clientContext.ExecuteQuery();

    foreach (User siteUser in users)
    {
        listOfUsers.Add(siteUser.LoginName);
    }

    foreach (List list in lists)
    {
        listOfLists.Add(list.Title);
    }
}
```

As you can see here, this is just simple CSOM code. Go ahead and run this app, you will be asked to provide your Office 365 credentials at this point, when you run the app, you will see the gets deployed in office 365, but when you use it, the AppWeb is actually running on your machine. This can be seen as below,

So how do we run it in azure? Easy! Right click\Publish your app.

Next, logon to the Admin area of your Office 365 site – if you are using the developer site template, you will find a link for "Admin" on the top right. Specifically, you will need to access the "SharePoint" area of the Admin area.

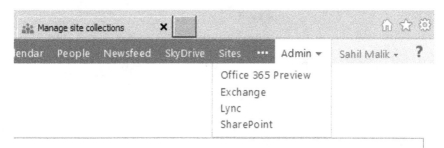

In the SharePoint admin area, look for the "Apps" section, and click on "App catalog" to the right,

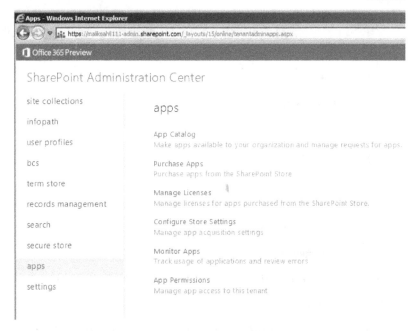

In the "App catalog" area, click on "Apps for SharePoint" and add your .app file that you published a moment ago from Visual Studio. This can be seen as below,

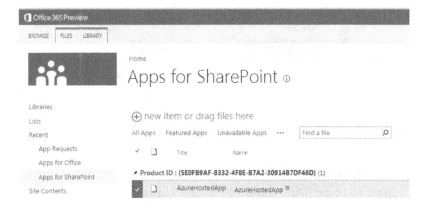

Now visit your Office 365 SharePoint online site again, and go to the "Site Contents" area, click on the "Add on app" button, and locate your new "AzureHostedApp" as shown below,

Apps you can add   Newest   Name

AzureHostedApp   Document Library   Form Library   Wiki Page Library
App Details   App Details   App Details   App Details

You will be asked to trust this app as shown below,

Do you trust AzureHostedApp?   ✕

Let it read items in this site.

Let it access basic information about the users of this site.

AzureHostedApp

Trust It   Cancel

Once the app is trusted and installed, go ahead and launch it.

You will see that the app runs just like before,

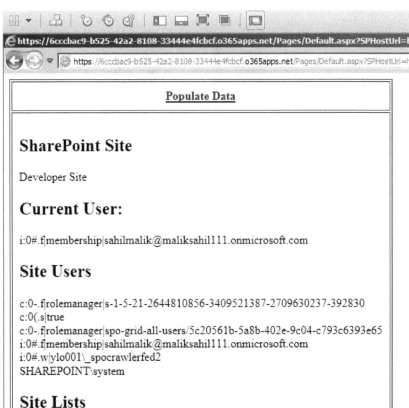

But note the URL this time around!

https://6cccbac9-b525-42a2-8108-
33444e4fcbcf.**o365apps.net**/Pages/Default.aspx?SPHostUrl=
<<remove>>

The App is now running in Azure!! WOOHOO!! This is quite a big deal really, you didn't have to create the backend site, it was created for you – when the app was installed. This also is a good excuse for me to point a limitation of azure hosted apps – that an azure area is created for you whenever the app is installed. If the app is installed 50 times, you will get 50 such areas. So if you want to have a further fine grained control, perhaps a provider hosted app is a better choice for you. But in many circumstances, the convenience of an Azure hosted app is hard to beat.

I'd recommend you go ahead and uninstall the App if you're not using it, just so you don't end up getting charged for it.

End Exercise: Writing apps for Office 365

Congratulations, you have written an Office 365 app. That leaves me with just one more thing to describe before wrapping this up. And that is On the fly permissions.

App Only Permission policy

As I mentioned earlier in this book, permissions are of three types,

a) User only
b) User + App
c) App only

Lets look deeper into App only policy. This is where you don't have a user's identity, or the currently logged in user's identity is not enough to perform a certain action, and you need to elevate via the App. Remember, such an app can only be installed by the site collection administrator.

The assumption is that you have already written a Provider Hosted app, and you feel quite comfortable writing another one. So first, go ahead and setup a provider hosted app that you can successfully run and deploy from Visual Studio. The default code from the Visual Studio template app when written will simply show you the title of the SPWeb. Remember, this is a provider hosted app. Once you have that much working proceed with the exercise below.

Begin Exercise: App Only security policy

Assuming you have a provider hosted app that displays the title of an SPWeb, Next, I will enhance it to use App Only Security Policy.

The idea here is that our app wishes to do something – change the title of the SPWeb. But, you cannot do that unless you have Full Control permission. But we have a user in the SPWeb called "croc", and croc has only read permissions. However you will see that Croc will be able to change the title of the site using this app.

In order to do so, you need to do three things,

a) Change the permissions of the app so it requests Full Control on the SPWeb
b) Change the app so that it requests App only permissions policy
c) Change the logic of the app so it changes the title of the SPWeb.

So lets get started, change the permissions of the app as shown below,

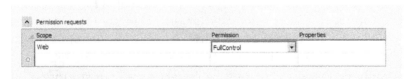

In AppManifest.xml add the following attribute -
AllowAppOnlyPolicy="true"

```
</Appriincipai>
  <AppPermissionRequests AllowAppOnlyPolicy="true">
    <AppPermissionRequest Scope="http://sharepoint/content/sitecollection/web" Right="FullControl" />
  </AppPermissionRequests>
</App>
```

Finally in the Default.aspx.cs of the App, add the following
code.

```
protected void Page_Load(object sender, EventArgs e)
{
    // The following code gets the client context and Title property by using TokenHelper.
    // To access other properties, you may need to request permissions on the host web.

    Uri hostWeb = new Uri(Request.QueryString["SPHostUrl"]);

    using (var clientContext = TokenHelper.GetS2SClientContextWithWindowsIdentity(hostWeb, Request.LogonUserIdentity))
    {
        clientContext.Load(clientContext.Web, web => web.Title);
        clientContext.ExecuteQuery();
        Response.Write(clientContext.Web.Title);
        clientContext.Web.Title = DateTime.Now.ToLongTimeString();
        clientContext.Web.Update();
        clientContext.ExecuteQuery();
    }
}
```

Now go ahead and deploy the app from visual studio. You
will probably have to sign in as administrator to SharePoint.

Verify that after the app has run once, the Title of the
SPWeb changes from "Test" to the current time as shown
below,

Keep Visual Studio running, and open chrome browser, and
login to http://sp using croc (you may have to add croc into
the site as a read only user).

Once you have logged in as Croc, locate your installed app

Still logged in as Croc, launch the app – the app simply shows you the current title,

But, now view the title of the SPWeb in another window – either as administrator or croc, verify that the title has changed,

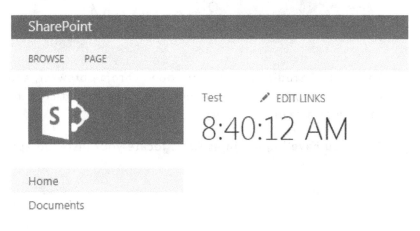

So you can see, croc was able to elevate his rights and do things through the app that he didn't have permissions to do as a user.

End Exercise: App Only security policy

Now can you guess why app only permissions are not allowed in JavaScript code? I did mention it earlier in the book. Think security!

On the fly permissions

All through the book I said, the developer specifies the permissions required for an App, and during the installation of the App, the user grants permissions for the App.

There is one exception to this rule. And that is on the fly permissions. The way on the fly permissions work is that your app gets installed with certain permission rights. It can do most of whatever it needs to do under the provided access rights. But a particular action requires elevated permissions. The app can request higher permissions on the fly.

This is actually a very useful capability to have for two reasons,

a) Your app can now be installed under much lower permissions required; this means more users will feel comfortable installing it.
b) Certain permissions, such as full control are explicitly blocked when submitting to the marketplace, but they are perfectly all right when requested on the fly. This means, your app when it wishes to find out a particular list URL, can temporarily elevate its

permissions. Users will also feel comfortable doing this because they are only granting such permissions for a short period of time.

Here is how on the fly permissions work,

a) You have an action in your app that will say "Click here to request permissions from your SharePoint site" or something like that. Clicking that action will use a method called TokenHelper.GetAuthorizationUrl to request permission. TokenHelper.GetAuthorizationUrl inclues a redirectToUrl. This redirectToUrl must have been pre-registered with the SharePoint installation. Note that TokenHelper.GetAuthorizationUrl works only with OAuth and Azure ACS. The below code demonstrates this,

```
protected void Button1_Click(object sender, EventArgs e)
{
    string redirectToURL =
        Request.Url.Scheme + "://" + Request.Url.Authority + Request.ApplicationPath.TrimEnd('/') + "/Pages/Redirect.aspx";
    string authURL = TokenHelper.GetAuthorizationUrl("https://maliksahil111.sharepoint.com", "Web.Write", redirectToURL);
    Response.Redirect(authURL);
}
```

b) The user is then prompted with a chromeless page asking for permissions, The user needs to have the permission themselves to grant the requested permissions.

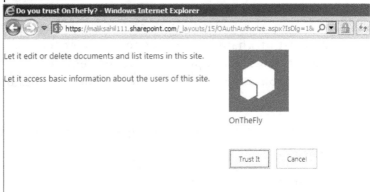

c) When the user clicks on the "Trust It" button, SharePoint returns an Authorization code, using which you can create an client context. Note that in the client context, I have hardcoded a GUID – that is the realm for Office 365 – that will never change, this is the special GUID for Office 365.

```
protected void Page_Load(object sender, EventArgs e)
{
    TokenHelper.TrustAllCertificates();
    string baseUrl = Request.Url.Scheme + "://" + Request.Url.Authority + Request.ApplicationPath.TrimEnd('/') + "/";
    Uri redirectURI = new Uri(baseUrl + "/Pages/Redirect.aspx");
    string authCode = Request.QueryString["code"];

    Uri targetSPUri = new Uri("https://maliksahilll.sharepoint.com");
    var tRealm = TokenHelper.GetRealmFromTargetUrl(targetSPUri);

    ClientContext context = TokenHelper.GetClientContextWithAuthorizationCode(
        "https://maliksahilll.sharepoint.com",
        "00000003-0000-0ff1-ce00-000000000000",
        authCode,
        tRealm,
        redirectURI
        );
}
```

Also, you see that I am using a method called
TokenHelper.GetRealmFromTargetUrl. This is a private
method by default. You will have to make it public to
extract the target Realm for your Office 365 site.
Please note that this realm doesn't change for your
site once it has been provisioned, so once you have
extracted this realm, mark the method private again
and hardcode it in your code (or make it configurable
via some means).

That's basically it, you have an on the fly app working.

Source Code

Thank you for reading this far. I'm guessing you are looking
for the source code for this book. You can find it at
http://sdrv.ms/YytNNB.

Summary

This book presents the biggest difference between
SharePoint 2010 and SharePoint 2013. It is also the
culmination of Microsoft's experience with SharePoint 2010
sandbox solutions, the larger community efforts in creating

OAuth and JavaScript based technologies and Microsoft's open embrace for those.

It is not a stretch to say that this book is the biggest fundamental building block of SharePoint 2013. It teaches you all the fundamentals of Apps, beyond here, you need to familiarize yourself with two key technologies to round up this knowledge. The first is the Client Object Model and REST API fundamentals, along with a further discussion on security. And the second is to simply familiarize yourself with the enhancements in the API (specifically the client side apis) that have been introduced in SharePoint 2013 in support of this App development philosophy.

Until then, be appsome, bon-appetit, and go ahead and inhabit the planet of apps.

www.ingramcontent.com/pod-product-compliance
Lightning Source LLC
Chambersburg PA
CBHW071202050326
40689CB00011B/2213